1-17-61

Behavior

Science

Monograph

ORGANIZATION
OF WORK

*a comparative analysis of production
among nonindustrial peoples*

Stanley H. Udy, Jr.

with an introduction by

George P. Murdock

HRAF PRESS NEW HAVEN 1959

1144081

TO MY PARENTS

THE EXTENT to which this monograph makes a contribution to the field of industrial sociology can be judged, of course, only by the author's professional colleagues in that field. It may also be weighed, however, as an exercise in the comparative method. On this score it is impressive. In addition to being substantively and methodologically sound, it has important implications for the use of the Human Relations Area Files in particular and for cross-cultural research in general.

Despite the common misconception of the Files as primarily an anthropological enterprise, the organization was actually established to serve equally the sister disciplines of geography, psychology, sociology, and human biology. This monograph, written by a sociologist and utilizing a conceptual framework derived exclusively from sociology and economics, demonstrates the utility of the Files for research in nonanthropological fields. It marks, moreover, a return to the great sociological tradition of comparative ethnographic research pursued by Spencer, Durkheim, Sumner, and numerous lesser figures of the past.

To revive this tradition fruitfully, the author has found it necessary to revise both the theoretical orientation and the methodology of his predecessors. He postulates no evolutionary sequences of development but formulates and tests hypotheses regarding functional interrelationships among coexisting organizational forms. Reacting also against extreme cultural relativism, he demonstrates that valid and significant results can emerge from the "comparative study of selected aspects of culture."

The author's methods contrast sharply with those of the earlier comparative sociologists. He surveys, not an indiscriminate body of ethnographic literature, but the sources on a carefully selected representative sample of nonindustrial societies. Instead of lifting cases out of their cultural context, he analyzes the interrelationships among his variables within each of his sample cultures. He carefully defines his variables in trans-cultural rather than in culture-bound terms. And he arrives at his conclusions by first formulating hypotheses and then testing them statistically against the discovered intra-cultural relationships, not by an intuitive assessment of excerpted materials.

The fact that sixty-four separate propositions have received impressive statistical confirmation bears witness to the author's sophistication in theory and method, and at the same time offers substantial encouragement to all social scientists interested in cross-cultural research. The author, who has had no formal anthropological training and only minimal anthropological guidance, demonstrates precisely thereby the way in which the Human Relations Area Files renders the vast riches of ethnography and culture history readily accessible to anyone with a scholarly interest in human behavior.

GEORGE P. MURDOCK

THE HUMAN RELATIONS AREA FILES

THE HUMAN RELATIONS AREA FILES is a nonprofit research corporation affiliated with Yale University and sponsored and supported by its sixteen member universities. HRAF was established in 1949 "to collect, organize, and distribute information of significance to the natural and social sciences and the humanities." It has concentrated upon furthering a fresh approach to the study of societies, culture, and social behavior.

The Files themselves contain carefully selected sources analyzed according to G. P. Murdock's *Outline of Cultural Materials*. Located at each of the member universities, they are a new kind of reference library in which basic information about nearly two hundred peoples can be consulted with ease and speed.

MEMBER UNIVERSITIES

University of Chicago
University of Colorado
Cornell University
Harvard University
University of Hawaii
Indiana University
State University of Iowa
University of Michigan

University of North Carolina
University of Oklahoma
University of Pennsylvania
Princeton University
University of Southern California
University of Utah
University of Washington
Yale University

IF SOCIOLOGY is to be a true science of human society, some effort, however imperfect and modest, should be made to achieve generalizations about social structure through comparative analysis. Essentially it is this conviction, combined with a specific interest in production systems, that has led me to attempt a comparative study of work organization on a cross-cultural basis. Over the years, a vast body of descriptive data about human society has accumulated in the form of anthropological monographs. Presumably one of the main reasons for collecting such data is to provide an empirical basis for generalization about social phenomena. Yet it is surprising how seldom ethnographic data are used for this purpose on a large scale. One of the objects of this study is to demonstrate, in a modest, and I hope reasonably successful way, that comparative analysis of ethnographic materials is a feasible and fruitful means of reaching sociological generalizations—in particular, generalizations about production systems.

The author owes a great debt to Professors Marion J. Levy, Jr., Wilbert E. Moore, and Melvin M. Tumin, of Princeton University, who directed the doctoral dissertation on which the present monograph is based.* An equally important debt is also due Professor George Peter Murdock of Yale University, not only intellectually for his work in comparative social analysis, but also for giving freely and patiently of his time in advice, suggestions, and material bibliographical assistance incident to revision of the original manuscript. The intellectual influence of these men will be apparent throughout in whatever merit this effort may possess;

---

* Udy, "The Organization of Production in Nonindustrial Culture." Unpublished doctoral dissertation, Department of Economics and Sociology, Princeton University, 1958. The present monograph is essentially a revision of this thesis.

for shortcomings and errors resulting from misapplication of their advice, or for any other errors, I am of course alone responsible. I also wish to thank Professors Theodore R. Anderson, Omar K. Moore, and Stephen W. Reed, together with Dr. Frank M. LeBar, all of Yale University, for valuable suggestions. In addition, Messrs. David Matza and Harrison C. White, former fellow graduate students at Princeton, have been extremely helpful in ways of which they themselves may not be fully aware.

Special gratitude is due Mrs. Katherine R. Cameron, Director of the Human Relations Area Files Section of the Firestone Library at Princeton University, where most of the research was carried out. Mrs. Cameron's efficient management of the Files and wholehearted cooperation enabled work to proceed at a much more rapid pace than would otherwise have been possible, and indeed made it possible to do some things which otherwise could not have been done.

STANLEY H. UDY, JR.
Yale University
New Haven, Connecticut
November, 1958

CONTENTS

LIST OF TABLES

ORGANIZATION OF WORK

PROBLEMS AND PROCEDURES

DESPITE THE FACT that comparative analysis has long been recognized as a legitimate means of discovering sociological principles, its current popularity as a method of research is less than notable.[1] There are, moreover, some very good reasons for this evident lack of vogue. Comparative analysis not only presupposes a considerable number of descriptive studies in the area to be researched, but also presumes that such studies are of a sufficiently uniform theoretical and methodological persuasion to render comparable the data presented. Conditions in this regard seem particularly discouraging in the field of industrial sociology, owing not so much to a paucity of case studies, but rather to a lack of comparability between them. The student interested in general propositions about industrial work organization is therefore faced with a lifetime of countless field studies, not to mention attendant difficulties of securing access to observe in each case, before he can even begin to develop his major interest by this method.

Ironically enough, this situation does not entirely apply to the study of nonindustrial production. Over a period of several decades a considerable amount of ethnographic data has been amassed on nonindustrial cultures by methods which admit of at least some minimum degree of comparability. The relatively recent development of the Human Relations Area Files and their expansion to workable proportions have, moreover, made comparative studies of rather broad scope quite practicable.[2] In such ethnographic materials, the student of work organization finds a wealth of descriptive data pertaining to his field of interest and relating to a variety of cultural contexts. It was felt that an attempt to analyze such materials with a view to generalization would be of some value. All work, whether nonindustrial or not, has certain common general features about which surprisingly little is known. For example, although it is well known in a general way that work organization structure is determined both by its cultural setting as well as by the technological features of the work being done, very little is specifically known about which features of organization structure are determined by technology irrespective of cultural setting, and which features are on the other hand culturally variable irrespective of technology. Again, one may be quite sure that the pattern of rewards for work depends both on kind of organization as well as the broader cultural setting, but which specific aspects of rewards are determined by organization structure as opposed to general culture is far from clear. Clarification of such matters would not only add to the general fund of knowledge of social organization, but would also be relevant to the study of development of underdeveloped areas and to industrial sociology per se. Furthermore, cross-cultural analysis of organizational forms is useful in establishing extreme limits of possible variation of such forms, and hence useful in developing administrative and organizational theory in more restricted settings.

This monograph, then, is a comparative study of the various ways in which different kinds of work are organized among nonindustrial peoples in the production of material goods. Such production may be carried on either by individual persons or by collectivities, and is found in some form in every known human society. This study, however, will be concerned only with collectively organized production systems in nonindustrial cultures, and will place particular emphasis on three aspects of this subject: technology, organization, and rewards. Primarily, the analysis will explore specific interrelationships between these elements, in their broader social setting. Two very general hypotheses have guided the research; they will be set forth presently, together with a discussion of the sources of empirical data and the methods of analysis employed.

Basic Concepts and Methods

Production is defined as the purposeful alteration and combination of physical material until it reaches some desired empirical state. Physical activities performed in connection with production constitute *work*.

Any collective production system involves a technological process carried on by a production organization, with a reward system, in a social setting. The term *technological process* refers to the system of physical operations performed on the material, and *production organization,* to any social group manifestly engaged in carrying on one or more such processes, at least some of the time. Such a group may or may not have other functions as well; their range and nature is left as a matter for empirical determination. A *reward* is defined as any material object which accrues to an individual or group as an institutionalized consequence of participation in a production organization; a *reward system* is that pattern according to which rewards are allocated among members of the organization.[3]

All production organizations exist within some society, and may further prove to be fully contained by some subgroup within a society. In this sense, all production organizations, technological processes, and reward systems function within a *social setting.* No production organization is functionally self-subsistent; as a bare minimum, all are ultimately dependent on the social setting for provision of raw materials and recruitment of personnel.

Essentially, then, this study seeks to discover the principal ways in which technology, production organization, reward systems, and social setting are interrelated. Two general hypotheses have guided the research:

A. *The structure of any production organization is determined partly by the characteristics of the technological process which it is carrying on, and partly by the social setting within which it exists.*

B. *The structure of any reward system is determined partly by the characteristics of the production organization involved, and partly by the social setting, within limits imposed by features of the technological process.*

In the form stated, these hypotheses appear rather obvious. The problem is not to test their validity as such, but rather to discover the specific ways in which, and the specific conditions under which, one alternative possibility holds true as opposed to another. For example, the fact that production organization depends both on technology and social setting is well known, but little is known about which specific aspects of organizational structure depend on technology, which depend on the social setting, and what specific features of technology and social setting are involved. The primary analysis, then, will be of interrelationships between subcategories of these basic concepts, organized around the above two hypotheses.

For purposes of the present study, both technological process and social setting are assumed to be given, and are treated as independent variables. Actually, of course, the range of available technological processes is limited by social factors just as is the range of available organizational forms. Consideration of the relationship between technology and society, however, lies outside the scope of this work.[4]

The empirical basis of this study is a comparative analysis of 150 nonindustrial production organizations, as reported in the ethnographic literature. Any comparative social analysis of this type immediately encounters two rather difficult problems of method. The first is the question of independence of the units of observation, inasmuch as diffusion is often an unknown quantity. Each of the 150 sample organizations studied here was drawn from a separate society, under the assumption—not entirely realistic, to be sure—that production organizations in different societies constitute independent entities, while those in the same society do not.[5] Having thus at best "disposed" of this problem, one next faces the difficulty of securing a sample known to be unbiased. It is obviously impossible to select societies at random, owing to unevenness in the source materials. The expedient of consciously selecting societies distributed as evenly as possible over world culture areas was therefore resorted to, using the selection criteria set forth by Murdock, such that a roughly equal number of societies was chosen from each of the six major culture areas which he delineates.[6] To secure something approaching an even distribution within each area, the attempt was made to use no fewer than two and no more than four societies from each sub-area. Beyond this, the societies chosen were those on which the material available seemed the most reliable and complete. The result was a "quota" sample of 150 societies roughly stratified by culture area, as follows:

AFRICA

Ashanti	Hottentot	Nupe
Azande	Ila	Nyoro
Bemba	Jukun	Otoro
Boloki	Kikuyu	Sotho
Chagga	Kipsigis	Tallensi
Chiga	Lobi	Thonga
Dahomeans	Mbundu	Tiv
Dogon	Naron	Turkana
Fang	Nuer	Zulu

CIRCUM-MEDITERRANEAN

Babylonians (2000 B.C.)	Lapps	Saxons (900 A.D.)
Bedouin	Megrelians	Somali
English (1100 A.D.)	Mzab	Songhai
Germans (medieval)	Osset	Tigre
Hutsul	Riffians	Tuareg
Kabyles	Romans (Imperial)	Wolof

EAST EURASIA

Afghans	Chukchee	Malay
Andamanese	Dard	Maria Gond
Betsileo	Gilyak	Muong
Bhotiyas	Hazara	Samoyed
Burmese	Iranians	Semang
Burusho	Karen	Telugu
Cambodians	Kashmiri	Thai
Chinese (Shantung)	Kazak	Tibetans
Chiru	Li	

INSULAR PACIFIC

Aranda	Kiwai	Murngin
Atayal	Maanyan	Pukapukans
Belu	Macassarese	Samoans
Bisayan	Malekulans	Tahitians
Buka	Mangaians	Tikopia
Fijians	Maori	Trobrianders
Iban	Marshallese	Wogeo
Ifaluk	Mount Hagen Tribes	Yami
Ifugao		

6

Aleut	Kwakiutl	Sinkaietk
Blackfoot	Maricopa	Taos
Coeur d'Alene	Menomini	Tarahumara
Copper Eskimo	Navaho	Tarasco
Crow	Ojibwa	Tubatulabal
Flathead	Paiute (Northern)	Winnebago
Haida	Papago	Wintun
Havasupai	Patwin	Yaqui (Sonora)
Hidatsa	Penobscot	Yokuts
Hopi	Popoluca	Zuni
Iroquois	Sanpoil	

SOUTH AMERICA

Abipon	Cuna	Tenetehara
Apalai	Haitians	Terena
Aymara	Jivaro	Timbira
Cagaba	Mam	Trumai
Caingang	Nambicuara	Tupinamba
Camayura	Ona	Wapishana
Carib (Barama River)	Siriono	Yagua
Cayapa		

From ethnographic sources on each of these 150 societies, material was abstracted on 426 clearly reported production organizations and classified according to the conceptual framework which will be developed as the discussion progresses. The Human Relations Area Files proved invaluable and were utilized whenever possible.

From these 426 cases, one case was drawn at random from each society, with the exception that the sample was stratified so as to include an approximately equal number of organizations of each of seven major technological types to be defined in the next chapter. This sample was utilized in all statistical tests unless otherwise specified.

Thus in the majority of instances conclusions are based on a sample of 150 production organizations representing 150 different societies. These conclusions are stated in the form of propositions, and are demonstrated by simple statistical procedures.[7] Detailed examples given in the course of verbal discussion, however, are not necessarily restricted to these 150 sample cases. Also, in all statistical tests, cases lacking data on the matters at hand were dropped; unless otherwise noted, this procedure did not result in an upset of the over-all distribution by culture area.

It seems necessary to point out that the methodological problems of observational independence and sample bias are in no way related to the use of statistical procedures, but are common to all studies of this type whether statistical procedures are used or not. Implicit in the statement of any general relationship reached through the examination of a number of cases by whatever method is the contention that the relationship observed did not occur by chance. The use of statistical procedures does nothing more than make this contention explicit and in itself introduces no additional problems or assumptions provided appropriate techniques are employed.

Wherever possible, the Human Relations Area Files were employed in gathering data, and their availability materially shortened the research task. With the aim of locating descriptions of collective production, the following categories, as set up in the Files, were searched:

22. Food quest
23. Animal husbandry
24. Agriculture
31. Exploitative activities
32. Processing of basic materials
33. Building and construction
342. Dwellings
46. Labor
47. Business and industrial organization

Categories 46 and 47 were used mainly as checks on the procedure, for in principle every form of organized work reported for the society will be at least alluded to in the data indexed under these categories. Generally, however, work is described in detail under the appropriate functional category. Any kind of work mentioned under categories 46 and 47 not described under any of the other categories above was investigated in detail by consulting whatever other category was appropriate.

Social influences alluded to in the material on production were then followed up by consulting the appropriate institutional category in the Files. The following institutional categories were consulted especially often in this connection:

59. Kinship   62. Community
60. Family   64. Government

Category 62, "Community," was always consulted as a matter of course, since it usually includes some information on all sub-groups reported to affect life in the locality group. In many instances it contained all of the societal information needed; recruitment of membership and operational consequences of non-industrial production systems do not as a rule extend far beyond the bounds of the locality group. Other categories, however, were consulted whenever the data indicated that it was appropriate to do so, including categories other than the ones listed above, such as those dealing with religious institutions and voluntary associations.

NOTES TO CHAPTER ONE

1. Perhaps the best-known recent example of the use of this method is Murdock, *Social Structure*. Also see Apple, "The Social Structure of Grandparenthood," *American Anthropologist*, LVIII (1956); Davie, *The Evolution of War*; Driver, *An Integration of Functional, Evolutionary, and Historical Theory by Means of Correlations*; Freeman and Winch, "Societal Complexity: An Empirical Test of a Typology of Societies," *American Journal of Sociology*, LXII (1957); Goode, *Religion among the Primitives*; Hobhouse, Wheeler, and Ginsberg, *The Material Culture and Social Institutions of the Simpler Peoples*; Levy, *The Structure of Society*; Lewis, "Comparisons in Cultural Anthropology," *Yearbook of Anthropology* (1955); Murdock, "World Ethnographic Sample," *American Anthropologist*, LIX (1957); Salisbury, "Asymmetrical Marriage Systems," *American Anthropologist*, LVIII (1956); Schuessler and Driver, "A Factor Analysis of Sixteen Primitive Societies," *American Sociological Review*, XXI (1956); Simmons, *The Role of the Aged in Primitive Society*; Sumner and Keller, *The Science of Society*; Whiting, "The Cross-cultural Method," in Linzey (ed.), *Handbook of Social Psychology*; Whiting and Child, *Child Training and Personality: A Cross-Cultural Study*. Many other older works in the classical "evolutionist" comparative tradition could of course be cited, such as Lippert's *Kulturgeschichte der Menschheit*. These earlier works, however, differ in many important respects from more recent efforts.

The only studies with which the author is familiar which deal with the cross-cultural analysis of work are Buxton, *Primitive Labour*; and Nieboer, *Slavery as an Industrial System*. Buxton's work is in the earlier "evolutionist" tradition, and stresses technology as such; it does not deal with organization specifically. On the other hand Nieboer's study—which, as one may imagine deals with "slavery" more than with "work"—may quite accurately be termed cross-cultural. Furthermore, this remarkable and impressive work is, in general, more "functionalist" than "evolutionist" in orientation, despite the fact that it was written in the late nineteenth century; for its time, Nieboer's approach was virtually unique.

2. For a discussion of the Human Relations Area Files see Murdock, *et al., Outline of Cultural Materials.*

3. It would be highly desirable to consider certain nonmaterial items here, such as enhanced status. The attempt to do so, however, had to be abandoned owing to a lack of adequate cross-cultural data.

4. This subject has, moreover, been extensively treated in the literature. For only a few such examples see Forde, *Habitat, Economy, and Society;* Thurnwald, *Economics in Primitive Communities;* Viljoen, *The Economics of Primitive Peoples;* relevant sections of Hobhouse, Wheeler, and Ginsberg, *The Material Culture and Social Institutions of the Simpler Peoples;* and Cottrell, *Energy and Society.*

5. "Separate" societies were deemed to be those designated as distinct in Murdock, *Outline of World Cultures.*

6. See Murdock, "World Ethnographic Sample," *American Anthropologist,* LIX (1957).

7. The .05 level of significance was set as the criterion for rejections of null hypotheses, except in instances where not only the relationship itself but also the specific expectation that it would be very weak could be deduced independently from known facts. In such cases, null hypotheses were rejected at the .10 level.

2

NONINDUSTRIAL TECHNOLOGY

FOR PURPOSES OF THIS STUDY it will be assumed that all technological processes, whether industrial or not, have certain analytic features in common: complexity, work load, outlay, and uncertainty. In addition, processes may be classified concretely according to type of product. On this score a more or less standard scheme is employed, yielding seven types of nonindustrial production: tillage, hunting, fishing, collection, construction, animal husbandry, and manufacturing.[1] The four analytic "dimensions" of technology may then, as it were, be used as "base lines" for the comparative analysis of these seven concrete types, with a view to isolating technological variables which may prove to be predictive of organizational characteristics.

Types of Technological Process

The seven general types of nonindustrial production distinguished above are operationally defined as follows:

Tillage: all activities on the soil or the crop in connection with agriculture, up to and including storage of the crop for consumption, and including such operations as are performed with the aid of animal power. Irrigating soil, as an activity, is included here, but construction and maintenance of irrigation works is included under the heading "construction."

Hunting: the chase of land animals, including sea mammals (such as seals) when pursued on land.

Fishing: the gathering of any aquatic life form, except plants. This includes sea mammals when they are sought in the water as well as "fish" in the strict ichthyological definition.

Collection: the gathering of inanimate objects and plants already existing in the physical environment.

Construction: the building and maintenance of physical objects not generally considered portable. Included here, principally, are boats (any vessels designed to carry one or more persons on water), dwellings, communal houses, assembly halls, walls, trails and roads, and capital equipment.

Animal husbandry: all activities involving physical contact with domesticated animals, and primarily concerned with their care, breeding, and the obtaining of produce from them. The use of animal power in tillage, construction, or manufacturing is not included here, but under the relevant category in question.

Manufacturing: the production and maintenance of objects normally considered portable.

Given processes sometimes crosscut two or more of the above categories. For example, manufacturing or construction may also involve collection of raw materials. In such cases the process is deemed to be oriented to the last activity carried on, provided the same production organization carries out all parts of the process. Otherwise, each part of the process is classified under the appropriate heading.

These seven types of process may now be compared in terms of the four dimensions set forth above. As will be evident, the data are by no means equally complete in all four areas.

Complexity

The *complexity* of any technological process depends on the way in which the work is divided up and combined in time and space. From this standpoint, any process may be subdivided into tasks and operations. A *task* comprises all work performed during one period of organizational assembly. In modern industrial manufacturing, the organization is usually assembled continuously so that no differentiation ordinarily occurs by task. Nonindustrial production, however, is often carried on by organizations which assemble, perform part of a process, disband, assemble again at a later date, perform more work, and so on until the process is completed. Such parts of processes constitute separate tasks, with each such task consisting of one or more *operations*. An *operation* is any physical action which leaves raw material in such a condition that it can remain untended without further changes taking place during the time required by the task at hand. Within any task, operations may be performed in succession or simultaneously. Simultaneously performed operations within one task will be said to be *specialized* relative to one another. And whenever the effort involved in performing any operation is exerted by several persons working in unison according to some established rhythm, *combined* effort will be said to be present.[2]

Tillage

From the standpoint of complexity, the principal difference between industrial and nonindustrial technology is that the former characteristically involves considerable specialization, while the latter involves relatively more task differentiation. Tillage is particularly notable in this regard, owing to its close relationship to the seasonal cycle, combined with the necessity of waiting for the crop to mature. At least three tasks are almost invariably involved: preparation of the field and planting; tending the crop while it matures; and harvesting and storage. This differentiation is, however, minimal, with a much greater number of tasks frequently present. If shifting agriculture of the slash-and-burn variety is practiced, for example, the activity of field preparation becomes broken down further. Brush must be cleared, left to dry, and then burned.[3] Various other consecutive operations—some of which could conceivably be specialized but are rarely reported as such—are generally interspersed here, such as piling branches and digging roots. Similarly, with fixed agriculture and the use of various types of equipment, field preparation may become more complex in different ways. Plowing and hoeing often either become separated as tasks from planting or specialized as operations relative to planting. If irrigation is practiced, the added task of building and repairing works must be reckoned with.[4] Thus tillage is characterized by a relatively high degree of task complexity. Where the growing season is relatively long, with more than one crop involved, yearly tillage activities may assume the character of a rather complex program, as Tables I and II illustrate:

TABLE I
CALENDAR OF WORK IN CENTRAL CHINESE AGRICULTURE[5]

Month	Work Required
Feb Mar Apr	sowing seeds for rice, collecting and threshing broad beans
May Jun Jul Aug Sep	breaking soil, irrigating, mending dikes, adding fertilizer, leveling the rice-field, plowing, transplanting rice, weeding, three times
Oct	reaping, threshing, transportation
Nov	digging trenches for broad beans, sowing
Dec Jan	transportation of straw, and storage

TABLE II
CALENDAR OF WORK IN KASHMIRI AGRICULTURE[6]

Month	Work Required
Mar-Apr	Plow and manure for rice; plow for maize and other fall crops
Apr-May	Sow rice and maize; continue plowing
May-Jun	Same, and transplant rice seedlings
Jun-Jul	Harvest wheat and barley
Jul-Aug	Weed rice, maize, and cotton; harvest linseed
Aug-Sep	Same, and begin picking cotton
Sep-Oct	Harvest fall crops; if rain, plow for wheat and barley and sow wheat, barley, and rape-seed
Oct-Nov	Harvest rice; plow for wheat and barley
Nov-Dec	Plow for wheat and barley
Dec-Mar	Thresh rice and maize and other fall crops

14

The presence or absence of specialized operations in tillage is highly variable. Frequently a technological choice exists as to whether certain activities are to be specialized as operations or differentiated as tasks. The alternative selected often depends on the amount of time available for the activity. In this connection, wet ricefield cultivation offers some interesting variations:

> In wet ricefield cultivation, seedlings are raised in a nursery and subsequently transplanted into the main field. Dikes in the main field must be built and kept in repair. When the shoots are ready for transplanting, the mud in the main field must be brought to an even consistency and leveled. In some instances this is done by plowing the field several times; in others cattle are turned into it and driven around to stamp out the lumps of mud. The seedlings must then be removed from the nursery, transported to the main field, and planted. During all this period, water must be admitted to the main field in the proper quantity. All of these activities, furthermore, must be crowded into a period of a few days, to avoid damaging the crop. Thus, where this process is carried out on a large scale, a rather complex specialization often arises. Among the Betsileo, for example, removal of shoots from the nursery, transport of same to the main field, planting the shoots in the main field, driving cattle around in the field, pounding out lumps of clay with sticks, and regulating the flow of water are manifestly separated as six specialized operations making up one task. (The field-leveling party works ahead of the transplanting party, which follows along as the field is leveled). On the other hand, where the scale of the process is not so large, as with the Karen, similar activities tend more to be differentiated as separate tasks.[7]*

Crop tending does not usually involve much specialization. The activities of weeding, fencing, pest control, and water regulation are usually not carried out simultaneously, although at times they may be. Pressure of time here is not generally so great. Harvesting, on the other hand, often comprises a whole complex of operations bound up in one task owing to a shortage of time. Reaping, threshing, winnowing, and storing are the most usual set encountered, with specialization often present. Where another crop is to be planted in the same season, planting the second crop may also emerge as another specialized operation.[8]

---

* Examples given in small print do not constitute direct quotations unless enclosed in quotation marks.

Combined effort is also reported in tillage with some frequency. It often takes the form of hoeing or planting in rhythm,
frequently to the accompaniment of drums.

> In Haiti, a work organization called the *combite* is often
> used to assist in field preparation. Hoeing is done in unison
> according to a drum beat played by special drummers. Fre-
> quently the organization is divided into two or more squads,
> each under its own chief, with competition providing stimu-
> lation to greater effort.[9]

Thus tillage is characterized by a succession of seasonally determined tasks, with considerable specialization and combined
effort sometimes encountered.

Hunting

Typical tillage processes are likely to be repetitive in yearly
cycles, with each separate process lasting six months or even more.
Hunting processes are markedly different in these respects. To
be sure, some of them, such as the annual Plains Indian buffalo
hunts, take place only once a year, but hunting most frequently occurs as a short-term repetitive activity. Furthermore, single hunting
processes rarely last longer than a few days. Some may consume
only a few hours. Therefore only one task, or possibly two, is
generally involved, in contrast to the frequently rather complex
task structure of tillage.

As to specialization and combined effort, however, hunting
can be and often is equally as complex as tillage, and sometimes
more complex, depending on the specific method of hunting employed. The simplest method is essentially passive, with no special
attempt made to locate game. Traps, pitfalls, ambuscades, snares,
etc. are set up and tended as fixed facilities. The only operations
involved are gathering up the game periodically and transporting
it. Generally, this method is used only for hunting individual
animals.[10]

Of somewhat more interest are the "active" forms of hunting,
where direct manipulation of live game is involved. Again, processes are short with few tasks, but specialization is greater and
combined effort often present. Three "active" methods of collective hunting are common: driving, surrounding, and impounding.

Driving is used primarily against large herds. The game, once
located, is driven against some fixed obstacle—against equipment

of the sort used in passive hunting, as well as over cliffs, up box canyons, into lakes, etc. One task with several consecutive, non-specialized operations—such as preparing the equipment, locating the herd (if this has not already been done), driving it, killing the animals, and transporting them—is typical. Specialization is frequently present in that the obstacle is often manned while the game is driven against it; combined effort usually occurs in driving.

> Among the Tiv, a man experienced in bushcraft goes out after a rain. Upon seeing tracks, he walks in a circle until he returns to the same spot. If the animal has not come out of the brush, he notifies the village. A net is erected at the spot where the animal entered "because game always breaks back and comes out at the same point at which it went in." The group then moves around to the other side and drives the game into the net. Similarly, the Coeur d'Alene, in hunting deer herds split up into two parties; one group drove the deer against the other, who were stationed behind a barricade of sticks, from which the deer could be killed.[11]

Surrounding, as opposed to driving against an obstacle, tends to be used more against smaller herds and individual animals. The basic principle, of course, is to encircle the game so that it cannot escape. Once this has been done, the hunters may either shoot at it from a distance, or close in with a direct attack en masse from all sides. Encirclement by fire is sometimes used as a device to confuse the quarry or prevent its escape. As in the case of driving, few tasks are involved. Where a direct attack is made, combined effort is likely to be present, but otherwise not. Specialization also sometimes occurs in connection with the attack, as between maintaining an outer encircling ring, perhaps also building a fire, and attacking the animals.

> The Cuna hunt peccaries in groups of about twenty men who surround the game, hold it at bay with the help of dogs, and shoot at it. The Zulu hunt similarly, but without dogs, driving the game into the center from all sides and attacking them. The Azande surround elephants, holding them at bay with a fire (which also moves the elephants toward the center), and throwing spears from behind the fire. A small-scale variant is reported for the Copper Eskimo. Two men will stalk a deer "imitating" it. When the deer is about thirty yards away, one hunter hides while the other tries to maneu-

ver into a position to shoot the deer in such a way that if the deer bolts, the second hunter can get another shot.[12]

Impounding actually combines various features of driving and surrounding. A large number of animals are located and surrounded, then herded to some obstacle or corral, driven against or into it, killed, and transported. Considerable advance preparation is often required if a pound is to be built, with specialization and combination likely to take forms characteristic of construction per se. The hunting itself, as may be imagined, is likely to combine the complexities of both surrounds and drives.

> Plains Indian buffalo hunting often took place in this way. Parties of Blackfoot horsemen, for example, would herd buffalo from several miles distant into a fenced avenue, over a cliff, and into a pound below. After herding the buffalo to the beginning of the avenue, men would drive them from behind, while people stationed alongside the avenue shouted and waved, thus stampeding the buffalo over the cliff. The Crow used a similar method.
> The Thai, in an interesting variant, hunted wild elephants in this way by using trained elephants to herd and drive the wild ones into the pound.[13]

Hunting, therefore, is characterized by a very small number of tasks, with specialization and combined effort highly variable in complexity.

Fishing

Fishing is much similar to hunting as to complexity, with a small number of tasks, and the structure of operations and combined effort variable by type. Four basic methods of collective fishing appear common in this regard. The first is essentially passive, and involves the tending of fixed facilities, such as traps and weirs. Like its analog in hunting, this method is rather simple, minimally involving periodic gathering of the fish (usually as a routine matter) and transporting of them. Specialization and combination are ordinarily absent, except in some instances of continuous large-scale activities. For example, in Cambodia:

> "The coolies are divided into gangs. Each gang does only one sort of job. And each man in the gang does only one specific job. One man washes the fish. Another cuts off the

heads. A third rips open the catch, while a fifth man salts them."[14]

The equipment used appears generally to be constructed individualistically, or, if complicated, by some other organization than the one doing the fishing.

> A typical example is characteristic of Thailand, where the fish traps are built out into the sea in the form of radiating fences with funnels converging in a central rectangular structure, to which nets are fixed by cords. These traps are periodically visited by the fishermen. Among the Yakut, box traps are emptied every morning and the contents divided among the families of the village. Among the Burmese, *in* traps must must be rebuilt yearly at a cost of up to 5000 Rs., requiring the work of 20 men for about a month. Fish are gathered day and night on a rotational basis.[15]

The second method involves poisoning a pool and then grabbing the stupefied fish from it. This technique often appears to involve large numbers of people, and frequently assumes, at least in part, a recreational function. One task is involved, with the operations of preparing the poison and grabbing the fish consecutively separated and not ordinarily specialized, although where special equipment is used, poison preparation and readying the equipment may be specialized relative to each other. Combination of effort is rarely reported; on the contrary, grabbing the fish often seems to be characterized by much raucous disorder.

> Among the Atayal of Formosa, the Chief sets the day for fish poisoning. The poison is brought by a representative of each clan, is placed in the river, and "everyone" jumps in and grabs the fish. The Miao follow a similar procedure, but also dam the river. Some men build the dam, while others go for poison bark. Among the Carib, the "whole settlement" participates. The men build a fence across the water and poison is thrown in. The women, stationed by the fence, kill the fish with knives. The fish are then carried in baskets to a spot where they are eaten.[16]

The third method involves driving fish into a trap or net or against some obstacle. This is accomplished in one task with several operations, often with some specialization, where one group drives against another. Combined effort is ordinarily involved in making the drive. This method is usually carried out on a fairly large scale, with the process lasting up to one day.

A Jivaro fishing party is often divided up into two groups. One group drives the fish by splashing and throwing rocks, either into nets or against the shore where they are caught or harpooned by the other group. In a variant of this method, three men jump into the water and, holding a large net, move upstream, catching and grabbing fish and throwing them into a canoe following behind.

On Malekula, a number of men gather at a channel between the lagoon and the sea, and build a fence across the shallow part of the channel, forcing fish into the lagoon as the tide rises. Then one row of men drives the fish through the channel, and another row drives the fish into the shallow water by the fence.[17]

The fourth basic method of collective fishing involves surrounding or maneuvering the fish by coordinated action from several boats, additionally using nets, harpoons, tackle, etc. This technique is on the whole the most complex and the largest in scale, and is characteristic of collective offshore fishing. Considerable specialization is often required, together with combined effort.

In lift-net fishing in Malaya, one boat carries the net to and from the fishing ground and holds one corner while the net is being cast and hauled. Three other boats hold the other corners. The process is directed from a fifth boat, from which fish lures are also manipulated. A sixth boat helps carry the catch back.

In whaling among the Nootka, a number of canoes holding six to eight men each are used. The chief harpooner strikes, and others follow. When the harpoon strikes the whale, the line is cast off from the canoe and attached to inflated sealskins to keep the whale from diving. The carcass is then towed ashore by the entire fleet.

Porpoise fishing in the Solomon Islands combines various methods. Twelve to fifteen canoes are used. When porpoises are sighted, a priest signals with rattles, and the canoes surround the school. Another signal is given and all men shout and splash to drive the porpoises into the harbor and ashore.[18]

Collection

Collection is the simplest of all nonindustrial technological processes. Usually only a single task with no specialization is involved, and is carried out as a matter of daily routine:

> Collection of berries by the Aleut is carried on by groups of two to over five women, who go out to collect for periods lasting up to one day. Larger groups "make something of a picnic of it and may stay out all day, collecting, gossiping, planning for the next church holiday, and the like."[19]

Where success in collection is of more marginal importance, the process is likely to be less casual:

> Among the Aranda, collection takes place virtually continuously. In foraging, the group disperses, with members keeping track of one another's location by identifying footprints, and smoke-signals.[20]

Specialization, when it occurs, is not very complex. Among the Siriono, for example, men climb trees and throw wild fruit down to the women, who gather it up below.[21]

Occasionally collection involves a planned expedition to some definite locality. In such instances it is more complex, with preparations for the journey, transportation, and various ancillary services required.

> An annual expedition is made by the Zuni to gather salt from a dry lake bed some distance away. The expedition is arranged in July, announced four days in advance, lasts several days, and is surrounded by much preparation and ceremony.[22]

Construction

Construction is one of the most complex forms of nonindustrial production. As in the case of tillage, its major source of complexity lies in task differentiation, for construction lends itself to work in "stages," and is cumulative in nature. A considerable number of tasks is often involved, with the time periods between them shorter than in tillage, and considerable variation from task to task in work load and degree of specialization present. Much cross-cultural variation in detail is evident, as one might expect.

Kabyle housebuilding involves, first of all, the securing of raw materials. Wood, water, stones, and clay are obtained from different localities. They then must be transported to the site of construction. The next task involves preparation of the material. Bark is removed from trees, and timbers are fashioned. Stones are cut, and mortar is prepared from clay. Next the foundation is laid, usually by a professional mason and his assistants. Wall construction is rather complex. Stone blocks are carried to the mason. Women wet clay and pass it to one of the mason's assistants, who mixes mortar, using water carried to him by someone else. The mason places the stone blocks with the help of assistants; sometimes two crews work simultaneously on opposite walls. Next the roof is built, involving placement of posts, beams, rafters, and thatch. The door is then placed, and the interior arrangements made.

Among the Thonga and Tiv, housebuilding is less complex, but involves basically similar activities. The wall and roof however are built separately; a large number of men are required to move the roof to the walls and place it on the hut.

Canoe building in the Trobriand Islands involves, first of all, felling and trimming a tree, and transporting it. The next task consists of working the outside of the log into shape and scooping out the inside of the canoe. Prow-boards are then fixed, and the canoe is launched. This is followed by the rather complex task of erecting and fitting the gunwale planks and internal framework, lashing the planks, constructing the outrigger, and caulking; these operations are ordinarily specialized. Finally, the canoe is painted and a sail is made. Each separate task is inaugurated by a magical ceremony.[23]

Animal Husbandry and Manufacturing

Very little cross-cultural data were found as to complexity in animal husbandry or manufacturing. Basically involved in animal husbandry is taking the herd to pasture, tending it, bringing it back, and handling any emergencies that may arise, all on a routinized, repetitive basis.

Among the Chagga, cattle are taken out in the mid-morning, brought back at noon to drink and rest, and driven out again in the afternoon, until nightfall. Time is kept by observing the shadow of a stick set in the ground; boys not observing a set schedule are scolded or beaten. They are also required to take care lest the cattle stray on to another's land, or into cultivated fields.[24]

Herding becomes a bit more complex under conditions of migration or where roundups are necessary. Bhotiya herds, for example, are moved in charge of three or four drovers. Reindeer are rounded up by the Koryak by much the same method as hunting by impounding.[25]

Most of the literature on collective nonindustrial manufacturing seems either to be confined to Western economic history, to the description of techniques with little data on the social organization of work, or to simple allusion to the existence of such manufacturing with no further details. A typical example of the latter is a remark made by MacDonald, while discussing another subject, with reference to Tibet:

> "In each of the larger cities is a paper factory usually situated just outside the municipal limits, near a constant source of water. All operations in its manufacture are performed by hand." Monasteries also often "maintain their own paper-making staff."[26]

Rattray, for example, illustrates pottery manufacturing techniques among the Ashanti with a number of photographs which indicate that women work on pottery together in groups. No description, however, is given of work organization; the monograph in question does not purport to deal with that topic.[27]

Some exceptions to the above paucity of material exist, notably in the works of Cline and Wyckaert on iron forging in Africa, although the former is primarily concerned with technology per se.[28] Likewise, in various works on Western preindustrial economic history, some very complete descriptions are given of the social organization of work. Especially good in this respect is the work of Auscher on preindustrial French and Belgian porcelain manufacturing.[29] But, in general, available data on the social aspects of collective manufacturing appear inadequate for purposes of comparative institutional analysis, despite the existence of much data for some culture areas, and a plethora of excellent material on the purely technical aspects of nonindustrial processes.

Comparative Analysis of Complexity

As explained earlier, the three dimensions of complexity used here are task differentiation, specialization of operations, and presence or absence of combined effort. The total degree of complexity of any process will be defined by the expression:

$$C = T + O + E$$

where C = total degree of complexity, T = total number of tasks in the process, O = the maximum number of specialized operations ever present in any one task, and E = one or zero, depending on whether combined effort is ever present at any time in the process, or always absent, respectively. *Kind,* as opposed to degree, of complexity is defined by the relative values of T, O, and E. Thus processes may differ from one another both as to degree and kind of technological complexity. Comparative findings of the complexity of different types of processes are summarized in Table III for those sample cases where this information was available.

TABLE III*

DEGREE AND KIND OF COMPLEXITY
BY TYPE OF PROCESS

	$\overline{T}$	$\overline{O}$	$\overline{E}$	$\overline{C}$	Min. n
Tillage	3.85	2.31	0.61	5.83	12
Hunting	1.04	2.10	0.85	4.00	20
Fishing	1.23	2.05	0.50	3.42	14
Collection	1.22	1.55	0.11	2.88	9
Construction	2.94	2.18	0.40	6.10	10

On the basis of *t*-tests of the significance of differences in the above table, at the .05 level, the following propositions can be stated:

1.   *Tillage and construction are more complex in task structure than are hunting, fishing, and collection.*

2.   *Hunting is more complex with respect to combined effort than is fishing, collection, or construction.*

3.   *Tillage is more complex with respect to combined effort than is collection.*

With categories combined in a manner suggested by these findings, the following proposition also holds true:

4.   *In total degree of complexity, tillage and construction are more complex than hunting, and hunting is more complex than fishing or collection.*

---

* Sample altered at random to make maximum use of cases with these data available.

These findings, together with the lack of significant differences in specialization between types of process, suggest that the major source of complexity in nonindustrial production is task structure, rather than the ramified specialization characteristic of modern industry. However, if a process is defined as *simple* where C≤5, and *complex* where C>5, a comparison of simple with complex processes yields the values in Table IV.

TABLE IV*

SIMPLE AND COMPLEX NONINDUSTRIAL PROCESSES

	Simple			Complex		
	$\overline{T}$	$\overline{O}$	n	$\overline{T}$	$\overline{O}$	n
Tillage and construction	1.50	1.50	8	4.46	2.61	14
Hunting, fishing, collection	1.03	1.48	33	1.40	3.20	10

Not all relevant differences in this table are statistically significant, but the values suggest that, while it is true that complexity in tillage and construction is largely due to task structure, complexity in hunting, fishing, and collection, when it occurs, is due to specialization of operations. In this respect, tillage and construction as practiced in nonindustrial contexts appear to be further removed from industrial characteristics than do the other three types of production.

Work Load

Work load is defined as the distribution of effort over a process. Some processes require a more or less constant amount of effort; others require more effort at some stages of production than at others. Operationally, the distribution of effort over a process was roughly ascertained by observing variations in the numbers of people at work at different times. If persons are regularly added to or subtracted from an organization, the process involves a *variable* work load; if not, the work load is *constant*.

Variations in work load are closely related to task differentiation, in that the latter essentially "sets the stage" for the former, through reassembly of the organization at the start of each new

---

* Same sample as used in Table III.

task. In particular, a shortage of time allowable for completion of a task is likely to lead to a heavier work load. Tillage is especially subject to peak periods at planting and harvesting. In tropical regions, for example, field preparation and planting must usually be completed before the rains start; thus all personnel available are required. In harvesting, a similar problem is encountered in that the crop must be harvested after it matures yet before it rots. Insofar as work load is concerned, slack periods tend to occur between planting and harvesting.

> Fairly extreme examples of pressure of time leading to increased work load can readily be found in rice cultivation in the Far East. In central China, for instance, the period of abundant rainfall is often short, thus making it necessary to start and complete all plowing, harrowing, and sowing during a period of a few days following a rain, and requiring additional labor. Similarly, it is desirable that the crop be harvested within a week after it has ripened; this too requires additional labor. Between planting and harvesting the work load is less. Fei and Chang report much "seasonal wastage" of labor and indicate that the question of how this extra time can be utilized "becomes an important problem for the peasants." The Chiru provide a similar example of work load fluctuation. More than the usual amount of work is required in clearing, hoeing, plowing, and harvesting. In addition, weeding also takes place on a consolidated basis, all of it being done at once. Examples like these could be easily multiplied; the Hidatsa perhaps provide a rather typical situation of rather simple agricultural techniques, with heavier work loads during the planting and harvesting of corn.[30]

Construction is quite similar to tillage in this respect, but with variations perhaps less pronounced, and deriving more from the cumulative nature of the work than from seasonally determined time shortages. The case cited earlier from the Tiv, for example, illustrates an instance of assembling a building in parts, with large numbers of people subsequently required to put the parts together.[31] Transport of raw materials in the early stages of construction is also a frequent source of heavy work load.

In contrast to tillage and construction, hunting, fishing, and collection do not ordinarily involve great variations in work load within a single process, if only because processes are of relatively short duration and take place away from areas where auxiliary personnel would be available.

In Bedouin hunting, for example, the course of action is planned in an advance meeting of the chiefs, ordered by the sheikh. The hunting party starts out and is "self-contained" until it returns shortly thereafter; the work load remains constant, within the framework of a single task. The Flathead bison hunt takes place on a much larger scale, but in essentially the same way. The time is set, and all of the men take part, putting forth a maximum constant amount of effort over a short period.[32]

Collection and fishing are similar to hunting in this respect. Although the activity itself may be seasonal, fluctuations in work load do not normally occur within the framework of a single process. The following proposition therefore holds true:

5. *Tillage and construction tend to be characterized by variable work loads; hunting, fishing, and collection, by constant work loads.*

	Variable work load	Constant work load
Tillage and construction	43	8
Hunting, fishing, and collection	1	63

$$Q = +.99 \qquad X^2 = 78.81 \qquad P < .001$$

Outlay and Uncertainty

Inasmuch as the form of uncertainty present in a process depends in great part on the nature of the outlay, these two topics may be conveniently discussed together. For present purposes, *outlay* consists of land, fixed capital, and raw materials. Processes vary according to the gross amount of land required, as well as the intensity of its use. Tillage and construction require little land, but such land as is required is used very intensively in that it cannot normally be employed for any other purpose at the same time. In contrast, hunting and collection require considerable land, but do not involve intensive use.

When hunting buffalo, Crow hunting parties form a semicircle of horsemen, as large as twenty miles in diameter, to move the herd in the direction of the village, which is usually some distance away. The fact that the specific location of game varies also has important implications, among them being the requirement of a rather extensive area, all of which is never used at once, but any part of which could be used at any given time. Among the Dard, for example, men are especially appointed to scout the hunting territory, and send notice to the villagers when game is sighted.[33]

Thus a rather large area is necessary, especially in the case of hunting, if only because the precise location of game is variable. For the same reason, the area cannot be narrowly delimited. Relatively extensive land areas are required, all parts of which are not used simultaneously, but with free access necessary to any portion at any given time. Offshore fishing is quite similar, except of course that potentially competing forms of "land use" do not arise. Landlocked fishing, on the other hand, is often characterized by the use of fixed locations on a repetitive basis. Land requirements in animal husbandry are highly variable, depending on the type of animal and ecological conditions.

Processes also differ according to the extent to which fixed capital equipment is used at all, whether such equipment is permanent or temporary in nature, and whether or not it is constructed by the organization using it. Tillage is extremely variable in these respects. Draft animals and irrigation works appear to be the principal items of capital equipment involved. Whether or not they are employed at all is of course highly variable both culturally and ecologically. When they are employed, they may be regarded as relatively permanent and are generally raised or constructed by an organization different from the one using them, or by a person external to that organization.

Certain forms of large-scale hunting require considerable fixed capital outlay. Impounding, in particular, involves construction of a corral, usually in combination with various outlying fences. Such structures are ordinarily built by the hunting organization itself, and are usually designed for temporary use on one occasion only, with very few institutional ramifications.

> The Plains Indians often constructed pounds for the purpose of large-scale buffalo hunting. Apparently, there was no intention that the pounds would be used more than once. Other than the use of the pound itself, there appear to be no general technological or organizational differences between impounding and driving into a natural trap.[34]

Apart, possibly, from manufacturing—on which, along with animal husbandry, few comparative data appear to be available—

fishing is probably the most capital-intensive type of nonindustrial production. Although capital equipment can be very simple indeed, relatively complex and cumbersome equipment is frequently required, particularly when fishing involves collective effort. Such equipment is either immovable or may be moved only by dint of joint effort. Fixed traps, dams, and weirs, for example, must be built, kept in repair, and completely rebuilt at regular intervals—usually yearly, by the fishing organization itself. Boats and nets, on the other hand, are usually built by some organization other than the one doing the fishing. Such equipment is almost always regarded as permanent, and is often encumbered by complex institutional ramifications.

> Firth's well-known account of Malay fishing may be cited in this connection. Basically, a variety of types of boats are used, together with at least seven different kinds of nets. In Malaya, many of the institutional ramifications attached to these items center on the question of how the equipment is to be financed. Such equipment may be bought already built or it may be constructed; in addition, it may at times be borrowed rather than owned. If bought, the terms may be cash or credit. Ownership may be unitary or multiple. Borrowing of money or equipment immediately involves borrower-lender relationships which are often quite complex in that fish dealers, on whom fishermen are dependent for sale of produce, tend to monopolize control over capital. Relationships thus range from relatively free contract to extreme peonage, with attendant political complications.[35]

The nature of the raw material used and the form of uncertainty involved in a process are closely allied. In particular, two variables as to the character of the raw material appear relevant: the degree of emphasis in the process on purposeful manipulation of the material as opposed to leaving it alone to develop by itself, and the extent to which the raw material is itself subject to random behavior. In addition, one must distinguish between uncertainty inherent in the process itself, uncertainty as to influences of the setting on the process, and uncertainty as to the future use of the product. All types of processes involve some degree of uncertainty; it is in fact quite difficult to say whether one type is on the whole "more" or "less" uncertain than another. Processes do differ, however, as to characteristic ways in which the above variables are combined. Thus different *kinds* of uncertainty may be roughly distinguished, under the assumption that they are indicative of differences in attitude required toward the work. Consequently it is possible to indulge in some studied speculations, in these terms, as to the major problems characteristic of each type of process.

Tillage is quite distinctive in its relative emphasis on development of the raw material, as opposed to purposeful manipulation. This does not of course mean that crops are not manipulated, but simply that their own growth is also an integral part of the process to an extent not found elsewhere. Two important implications follow. First, the relative dependence on growth places much of the process beyond direct immediate human control of the sort, for example, found in construction. Secondly, a thorough understanding by the members of the production organization of that part of the process not under direct human control is not essential to successful production. It is only necessary that the members be able to set up the appropriate conditions for it. Production, in other words, can take place in the face of minimal scientific understanding of what is going on. To the degree that such understanding is in fact minimal, unpredicted behavior of the material resulting either from uncertainty inherent in the process or from external sources cannot be controlled or compensated for in a rational manner. The problem becomes one, rather, of social adjustment to such behavior. Furthermore, inasmuch as tillage processes are rather lengthy, the outlay is exposed to its setting for relatively long periods of time, and is thus subject to a maximum degree of uncertainty from external influences. Such influences may to some degree be regarded as random. Holding ecological conditions constant, however, the crops themselves are not particularly subject to random behavior. One may conclude, therefore, that uncertainty in tillage takes the form of more or less random external influences which must be accepted and adjusted to socially, in a probable context of minimal scientific understanding of the nature of the technological process.

Viewing uncertainty as reflected in the existence of magical practices, Malinowski finds that the Trobriand Islanders possess a sound, scientific understanding of the more certain aspects of agricultural production—soil properties, the effects of weather, the nature of different crops, and the like. Here he refers to the conditions surrounding crop growth. Such knowledge is not confused with magical practices. "The natives will never try to clean the soil by magic, to erect a fence or yam support by a rite." On the other hand, the actual growth of crops once these conditions have been met is felt to be dependent on magic, as is absence of external catastrophe. Failures not attributable to bad workmanship in agricultural preparations are thus explained and adjusted to in terms of magical lore.[36]

Hunting and fishing, and to a lesser extent collection, differ considerably from tillage in these respects. This, again, is not to say that they involve less uncertainty or less magic, but that the uncertainty and probable orientation of the magical practices are of a different kind. Purposeful manipulation is, in the first place, relatively more important than growth. In addition, the "raw material" is subject to random behavior of its own accord, in the sense, for example, that herds of wild game are usually constantly on the move, and are still subject to movement while they are being hunted. Purposeful manipulation, to be successful, depends upon a scientific understanding of the process. Here, however, it must take place in a context of random location of game, fish, or produce to be collected, and possible random behavior of game or fish once located. The problem is one, not of social adjustment to uncertainty, but of generating optimal random strategies to locate "material," and of paying strict attention to the process thereafter to permit ready physical adaptation to possible random behavior. And, to the degree that hunting, fishing, and collection processes are not lengthy, uncertainty of external influences is less likely. Thus, the only "insoluble" problem of uncertainty here is one of locating the material. Once game or fish have been found, uncertainty can be compensated for rationally, given strict attention and maximum scientific understanding.

> O. K. Moore points out that divination is widely diffused as a procedure in determining the direction to take in searching for game, and suggests that it acts as a decision-making mechanism which randomizes strategy. Speaking of scapulimancy among the Naskapi he argues that ". . . divination based on the reading of cracks and spots serves to break (or weaken) the causal nexus between final decisions about where to hunt and individual and group preferences in the matter."[37]

It may be suggested, therefore, that tillage differs from hunting, fishing, and collection both as to kind of uncertainty and form of ritual reaction to it. It is, however, impossible to maintain that some types of processes are "more uncertain" than others, or that they involve "more magic" than others, since the possible sources of uncertainty are varied and not necessarily correlative with one another. Construction, for example, is characterized by scientifically understood, purposeful manipulation of material which is subject neither to random behavior nor to severe external uncertainties. Yet the fact that constructed products are ordinarily expected to last for some time opens the door to uncertainty regarding their future use.

> Malinowski, for example, finds quite as much magic associated with canoe construction as with agriculture, in the Trobriand Islands. Magic in canoe building, however, appears to be largely oriented to future performance of the canoe, not to the process itself (as in agricultural "growth" magic), or to preventions of external events which might interfere with construction. Rites are performed, for instance, to ensure the speed and stability of the canoe, given good craftsmanship.[38]

Cutting across all these distinctions is another source of uncertainty: the frequent necessity for decisions which are essentially arbitrary from the standpoint of technology, but which are necessary on organizational grounds. An example would be a decision as to the precise time at which a process requiring a large work force is to start; some decision is necessary, but any alternative may be acceptable technologically. In general, such decisions are reached either through routinization or by analogy to some external event. The former is usual with short-cycle repetitive activity, as in emptying fish traps, taking herds to pasture, and some forms of foraging. Where yearly or seasonal cycles occur, as in tillage, analogy to external events is more likely. Some form of calendar often functions as an intervening standardization device. As on other occasions of adjustment to uncertainty, religion and magic are likely to be involved. Where processes are apt to be unique, as in construction or infrequent hunting expeditions, divination is common.

> As indicated in previous examples, Burmese fish traps are tended daily. Chagga herding is similarly routinized, as is Aranda collection. The Hopi carry on tillage activities with reference to a calendar. An hereditary religious official, the Sun Watcher, observes the relation of the sun to distant mountain peaks, and announces the periods of the seasonal cycle accordingly. Here, as in many other societies such as the Iroquois and the Trobriand Islanders, the calendar is reinforced by religious festivals, which inaugurate appropriate

agricultural tasks. Such cycles appear less clearly institutionalized in some cultures, such as the Bhotiyas. Here, planting
times are fixed by consulting astrologers.[39]

The preceding discussion is sufficient to show that the question of uncertainty is quite complicated. Qualitatively different
forms of uncertainty can be distinguished as characteristic of
different processes. However, it is difficult to say whether one
process involves "more" or "less" over-all uncertainty than another,
since the various dimensions of this phenomenon are not additive,
at the present stage of research. Common to all production situations is a necessity for some degree of planning in terms of
technical knowledge; in this sense production may be regarded
as a basically "rational" activity. Such planning, however, must
frequently take place in a context of random behavior of both
raw material and external setting, as well as imperfectly understood "growth." And to the extent that these factors cannot be
controlled, they must be adjusted to. In this sense, the traditional
notion of "rationality" becomes blurred.

Summary

Table V summarizes the modal characteristics of those types
of production offering sufficient numbers of cases to admit of
comparative analysis.

TABLE V
MODAL CHARACTERISTICS OF TECHNOLOGICAL PROCESSES

	Complexity	Work load	Land	Capital	Raw material and uncertainty
Tillage	Ct	V	S	Mp	G
Hunting	Ss	C	L	Mt	M
Fishing	Ss	C	M	Lp	M
Collection	So	C	L	So	N
Construction	Ct	V	S	So	P

Complexity: C = complex; S = simple; t = complexity when
present due to tasks; s = complexity due to specialization;
o = little or no complexity ever present.

Work load: V = variable; C = constant.

Land: S = small fixed secure areas; L = large areas with indeterminate access; M = mixed.

Capital equipment: S = small amounts or none; L = relatively great amounts; M = mixed; p = usually permanent; t = usually temporary; o = little or none used.

Raw materials and uncertainty: G = growth and tending, some randomness, production possible in absence of thorough understanding of process; M = manipulation with process understood in presence of randomness; N = manipulation with process understood, some randomness; P = manipulation with process understood, little or no randomness.

NOTES TO CHAPTER TWO

1. The sevenfold classification of types of production is essentially a combination of the classifications of Forde, Levy, and Murdock, *et al.* See Forde, *Habitat, Economy, and Society*, 361; Levy, *The Structure of Society*, 389-407; Murdock, *et al.*, *Outline of Cultural Materials*. Also see Bücher, *Industrial Evolution*, 83-149; Weber, *General Economic History*, 155-77; Gras, *Industrial Evolution*, 44. Limitations of space do not permit a detailed discussion of the derivation of the four analytic features of technology. Roughly, they were conceived in terms of the Parsons-Smelser theory of economic process to be a subdivision of the "technical production" aspect of the "production sub-system." See Parsons and Smelser, *Economy and Society*, 199. For the present, however, their justification can rest on pragmatic grounds. On the "analytic" vs. "concrete" distinction employed here in modified form, see Levy, *op. cit.*, 199-207.

2. Weber, *The Theory of Social and Economic Organization*, 225-6; Bücher, *op. cit.*, 252-80; Ireson and Grant (editors), *Handbook of Industrial Engineering and Management*, 291-2.

3. See for example Herskovits, *Life in a Haitian Valley*, 69-70; Provinse, "Cooperative Ricefield Cultivation among the Siang Dyaks of Central Borneo," *American Anthropologist*, XXXIX (1937), 77-80.

4. Compare Richards, *Land, Labour, and Diet in Northern Rhodesia*, 288 ff.; Hart, *Barrio Caticugan*, 280; Kenyatta, *Facing Mount Kenya*, 56-60; D. L. Lorimer, "The Supernatural in the Popular Belief of the Gilgit Religion," *Journal of the Royal Asiatic Society*, (1929), 211.

5. Adapted from Fei and Chang, *Earthbound China*, 22.

6. Adapted from Lawrence, *The Valley of Kashmir*, 326.

7. Hart, *op. cit.*, 303-19; Lawrence, *The Valley of Kashmir*, 330-1; DuBois, *Monographie des Betsileo*, 434-40; H. I. Marshall, *The Karen People of Burma*, 76 ff.

34

8. Hill, *The Agricultural and Hunting Methods of the Navaho Indians*, 39; Kenyatta, *op. cit.*, 55-60; Meek, *A Sudanese Kingdom*, 404-14; Quain, "The Iroquois," 250-1 in Mead (ed.), *Cooperation and Competition among Primitive Peoples;* E. O. Lorimer, "The Burusho of Hunza," *Antiquity*, XII, 135.

9. Herskovits, *loc. cit.*

10. Hill, *op. cit.*, 113-7; also, 96-182, for illustrations of almost all the techniques following as they are carried on by the Navaho.

11. East, *Akiga's Story*, 93-4; Teit, *The Salishan Tribes of the Western Plateau*, 101-3.

12. D. S. Marshall, *Cuna Folk*, 103; Kidd, *The Essential Kafir*, 315-20; Lagae, *Les Azande ou Niam-Niam*, 147-9; Schweinfurth, *The Heart of Africa*, 438; Jenness, *The Life of the Copper Eskimo*, 145-8; Stefansson, *The Stefansson-Anderson Arctic Expedition: Preliminary Ethnological Report*, 57.

13. Forde, *Habitat, Economy, and Society*, 45-68; Lowie, *The Religion of the Crow Indians*, 357-9; Srichandrakumara, "Adversaria of Elephant Hunting . . .," *Journal of the Siam Society*, XXIII, 68-9; Young, *The Kingdom of the Yellow Robe*, 397.

14. Brodrick, *Little Vehicle*, 149.

15. Young, *op. cit.*, 180-4; Graham, *Siam*, 39; Jochelson, *The Yakut*, 52; Orr, *Field Notes on the Burmese Standard of Living . . .*, 14-18.

16. Wiedfeldt, "Wirtschaftliche . . . Grundformen der Atayalen auf Formosa," *Mitteilungen der Deutschen Gesellschaft für Natur*, 15-16; Moninger, "The Hainanese Miao," *Journal of the North China Branch of the Royal Asiatic Society*, LII, 47; Gillin, *The Barama River Caribs of British Guiana*, 11-14.

17. Rivet, "Les Indiens Jibaros," *L'Anthropologie*, XVIII, 604; Up De Graff, *Head Hunters of the Amazon*, 209-10; Karsten, *The Head-Hunters of Western Amazonas*, 177; Deacon, *Malekula*, 191.

18. Firth, *Malay Fishermen*, 98-100; Forde, *op. cit.*, 77; Ivens, *The Island Builders of the Pacific*, 169-76.

19. Shade, "Ethnological Notes on the Aleuts," 32-3.

20. Chewings, *Back in the Stone Age*, 39-41; also see Basedow, *The Australian Aboriginal*, 148-9.

21. Holmberg, *Nomads of the Long Bow*, 28.

22. Stevenson, *The Zuni Indians*, 354-61.

23. Maunier, *La construction collective de la maison en Kabylie*, 22-62; Junod, *The Life of a South African Tribe*, I: 126; East, *op. cit.*, 53-55; Malinowski, *Argonauts of the Western Pacific*, 124-56, 415-16.

24. Raum, *Chaga Childhood*, 201-3.

25. Pant, *The Social Economy of the Himalayans*, 51-4; Kennan, *Tent Life in Siberia*, 185-6.

26. MacDonald, *The Land of the Lama*, 243.

27. Rattray, *Religion and Art in Ashanti*, 295-308, photographs.

28. Cline, *Mining and Metallurgy in Negro Africa;* Wyckaert, "For-

gerons païens et forgerons chretiens au Tanganika," *Anthropos,* IX, 371-80.

29. Auscher, *A History and Description of French Porcelain.* Also see Lipson, *History of the Woolen and Worsted Industries;* and Francotte, *L'Industrie dans la Grece ancienne.*

30. Shen, *Agricultural Resources of China,* 115; Fei and Chang, *op. cit.,* 144; J. C. Das, "Some Notes on the Economic and Agricultural Life of a Little Known Tribe on the Eastern Frontier of India." *Anthropos,* XXXII, 446-9; A. L. Wilson, *Agriculture of the Hidatsa Indians.*

31. Junod, *loc. cit.;* East, *loc. cit.*

32. Raswan, *Black Tents of Arabia,* 163-5; Turney-High, *The Flathead Indians of Montana,* 115-20.

33. Lowie, *The Religion of the Crow Indians,* 357-9; Leitner, *Dardistan in 1866, 1886, and 1893,* 34

34. Forde, *op. cit.,* 45-68.

35. Firth, *Malay Fishermen,* 47-93.

36. Malinowski, *Coral Gardens and Their Magic,* esp. p. 76.

37. O. K. Moore, "Divination—a New Perspective," *American Anthropologist,* LIX (1957), 69-74.

38. Malinowski, *loc. cit.* and *Argonauts of the Western Pacific,* 115-6.

39. Orr, *op. cit.,* 14-8, Raum, *loc. cit.;* Forde, *op. cit.,* 220 ff.; Morgan, *League of the Ho-De-No-Sau-Nee, passim;* Malinowski, *loc. cit.*

1144081

3

TECHNOLOGY AND ORGANIZATION

IT WILL BE ASSUMED HERE that the attributes of authority, division of labor, solidarity, proprietorship, and recruitment are common to all production organizations.[1] *Authority* is defined as institutionalized power of given individuals over the actions of others, with "power" understood in this context as the ability to influence actions of others in accordance with given ends.[2] By *division of labor* is meant role differentiation on the basis of production. Degree of *solidarity* refers to the relative precedence of organizational relationships over other similar relationships and broader social commitments.[3] *Proprietorship* is defined as the right to control possession of outlay. *Recruitment* refers to that process by which individuals become members of production organizations; a *member* is defined as any person incumbent to a role differentiated by division of labor.

As alleged earlier, the precise status of any of the above features is determined both by technology and social setting. The present discussion will be devoted to the impact of technology on organization structure.

Authority and Bureaucracy

Like all formal structures, production organizations have announced objectives, the realization of which depends upon the effective coordination of work. The structure of authority is at least highly strategic, and probably crucial, in securing such coordination. Two basic types of authority structure may be distinguished: *associational* and *bureaucratic*. An *association* is defined as a production organization with an active core of leaders and a passive periphery of followers such that action of the followers is influenced by the action of the leaders in all matters relating to production. A *bureaucracy* is defined as a production organization having three or more levels of authority such that the members on one level are subject to the authority of those on the next higher level, and so on.[4] All members who are an equal number of positions removed from the top of the hierarchy will be considered to occupy the same *authority level;* any member above the lowest authority level will be termed a *manager.*

Using the measure of complexity advanced earlier, one would infer that more complex processes tend toward bureaucracy, while simpler ones tend toward association. In this respect, it may be asserted that:

6. *Construction organizations are relatively more likely to be bureaucratic than are organizations carrying on other processes.*

	Bureaucracy	Association
Construction	11	7
Other	21	39

$$Q = + .48 \qquad X^2 = 2.89 \qquad P < .10$$

This relationship, however, is dubious and rather weak. Furthermore, tillage, which tends to be rather complex, cannot be shown to be particularly likely to be bureaucratic. Thus one must search for a more direct relationship between complexity and bureaucracy. The literature on administrative theory indicates that the number of roles which must be differentiated on the basis of authority in an organization is determined by limitations on the possible effective span of control—the number of individuals that can be effectively supervised by one person. It is frequently held, implicitly, that span-of-control limitations stem from limits on the number of qualitatively different items to which a supervisor can give his attention at one time. Thus Moore points out that the span of control varies directly with the uniformity of functions of subordinates and inversely with the number of problems regularly referred to the administrator for decision.[5] And Graicunas proceeds under the assumption that each social relationship between subordinates constitutes a potential "item" to which attention must be given by the supervisor.[6]

What, then, is the maximum number of different items to which a human being can give his attention at one time? On the basis of experimental psychological evidence, Urwick gives six as this number. Under the assumption that each individual supervised constitutes such an item, Hamilton also gives six. Similarly, deJong gives five, Kendall five, Davis alleges three to seven, and Dale, three to six.[7] The maximum number consistently alleged by all of these writers is five. For want of a more sophisticated procedure, five was therefore assumed to be a valid estimate of the upper limit of the "span of attention," on the basis of available theoretical literature.

The earlier analysis of technological complexity suggests that items to which attention must be given in any production organization consist of specialized operations, differentiated tasks, and maintenance of combined effort. For specialized operations involve control of differentiated work roles, tasks involve adjustments in organization structure, and combined effort involves coordinated rhythm. Assuming five, then, as the upper limit of the span of attention, and allowing an extra unit for possible uncertainty, one may state the following proposition:

7. *Organizations carrying on complex processes tend to be bureaucratic whereas organizations carrying on simple processes tend to be associational.*[8]

	Bureaucracy	Association
Complex process	20	2
Simple process	2	30

$$Q = +.98 \qquad X^2 = 35.27 \qquad P < .001$$

It will be recalled that a complex process has been defined as one in which $C>5$, and a simple one, one in which $C\leq5$.

Thus there exists a striking relationship between technological complexity and authority structure, which appears to hold independently of type of process or social setting. Technological complexity seems to lead to bureaucratic structure in nonindustrial systems in much the same way as in industrial systems. However, as has already been shown, the *kind* of complexity involved is often different. How does this affect the type of bureaucracy developed?

In some respects, nonindustrial bureaucracies tend to partake of properties commonly associated with "rational" administrative organization. The latter is characterized, among other things, by a specialized administrative staff which does not "work" in the sense in which that term is used here; by distribution of rewards for services by the organization to its members; and by rewards fixed according to organization office.[9] Similarly, in nonindustrial systems:

8. *In bureaucracies, managers are likely not to work, while in associations managers are likely to work.*

	Managers do not work	Managers work
Bureaucracy	8	2
Association	17	38

$$Q = +.79 \qquad X^2 = 6.66 \qquad P < .01$$

9. *Bureaucracies are more likely than associations to distribute rewards to members.*

	Rewards distributed to members	Rewards not distributed to members
Bureaucracy	23	3
Association	22	15

$$Q = +.67 \qquad X^2 = 3.65 \qquad P < .10$$

10. *In organizations where rewards are distributed to members, the quantity of the reward tends to vary according to organization office in bureaucracies, but not in associations.*

	Rewards based on office	Rewards not based on office
Bureaucracy	17	7
Association	7	25

$$Q = +.79 \qquad X^2 = 11.49 \qquad P < .001$$

In other respects, however, nonindustrial bureaucracies seem quite unlike the "rational" industrial type. In particular, they do not significantly involve rewards based on achievement, nor are they significantly likely to have specific single, as opposed to diffuse multiple, objectives.

	Rewards based on achievement in any respect	Rewards not based on achievement
Bureaucracy	4	19
Association	8	26

$$Q = -.18 \qquad X^2 = 0.05 \qquad P > .70$$

	Specific single objective	Diffuse multiple objectives
Bureaucracy	9	23
Association	17	26

$$Q = -.25 \qquad X^2 = 0.62 \qquad P > .30$$

There exists some quite scanty evidence, however, for certain rather intriguing patterns revolving around the question of functional specificity internal to nonindustrial bureaucracy. Where more than one manager occupies the same level of authority, the question arises as to which workers are responsible to which manager. Available examples suggest that where specialization is not present, certain persons are simply consistently subordinate to the same manager. Where specialization is present, however, there appears to be some tendency for managerial roles to be defined by activity supervised rather than by persons supervised. The worker is subordinate to whichever manager is in charge of the particular activity which the worker happens to be performing at the time. Thus some tendency seems evident toward "functional" organization approximating the sort proposed by F. W. Taylor in the early "scientific management" movement, rather than the straight line, "military" type.[10]

> In dwelling construction among the Kabyles, workers are responsible to the mason in matters of placing stones; in other matters they are responsible to the owner of the dwelling or his representative. In whaling among the Aleut, responsibility is often owed to one individual in matters of navigation and boat handling, and to another in matters directly related to landing the whale. Impounding of buffalo among the Plains Indians often involves divided responsibility as to preparation of the corral and scouting for buffalo. General maintenance of discipline is moreover typically entrusted to still another group in authority. In the preparation of wet ricefields for planting among the Betsileo, responsibility is owed to the old men of the community in matters of dike maintenance and drainage and, in matters of field preparation, to owners of the cattle being driven around in the wet field to stamp out lumps of soil to an even consistency; over-all authority rests with the owner of the field.[11]

The above examples are simply proposed as suggestive; this hypothesis cannot be demonstrated in a general way owing to the lack of a sufficient number of clear examples.

From the preceding analysis, it may be concluded that while bureaucracy tends to result from technological complexity, such complexity in itself does not necessarily produce all of the trappings of "rational" administration. In particular, complexity resulting from task structure does not. The ensuing discussion will pursue this problem further.

Division of Labor

One may speak of the amount, the basis, and the content of division of labor in any production organization.

The *amount* of division of labor present is equal to the maximum number of specialized operations ever performed at one time plus the total number of managerial roles which do not involve work in the sense in which that term is used here. Some interrelationship is apparent between these two elements. The fact that managers are less likely to work in bureaucracies than in associations (proposition 8) suggests that the greater the amount of authority of a position, the higher the probability that it will involve purely administrative as opposed to physical labor. Similarly, the fact that over-all complexity is associated with bureaucracy (proposition 7) suggests that if tasks and combined effort are held constant, the greater the degree of specialization, the greater the number of levels of authority. Proposition 7, however, also indicates that tasks and combined effort are substitutive for specialization as determinants of authority structure. Unfortunately, lack of adequate data precludes further exploration of these matters at present. The possibility seems clear, however, of stating these relationships in more precise form.

By *basis* of division of labor is meant the criteria according to which roles are differentiated. Such criteria may be either organizational or societal as to source. Organizational criteria include technology, authority, and rewards. In other words, within a given production organization, one role may be differentiated from another by specialized operation, level of authority, amount and kind of reward, or some combination of these bases, the precise forms of which are likely to be peculiar to the organization concerned. In addition, roles may be differentiated by general societal criteria; namely, age, generation, sex, resources, power, and religion.[12] Propositions 7, 8, and 10 suggest that when a certain degree of complexity is reached, managerial roles become separated from work roles and division of labor tends to be supported by differentially distributed rewards. Relationships between organizational and societal bases of division of labor are intimately involved with reward systems, and will therefore be discussed later.[13]

The *content* of division of labor refers to the form of mutual role-expectations present. Such expectations may vary along at least two dimensions: specificity-diffuseness, and achievement-ascription. Division of labor content is deemed *specific* if organizational objectives are explicitly limited to material productive ends, and *diffuse* to the extent that other ends are additionally involved or where objectives are obscure. Whenever rewards for work depend in any respect at all on amount of work done or effort expended, *achievement* is considered to be emphasized; whenever rewards are consistently allocated independently of work or effort, evaluation of performance is said to be based on *ascription*.[14]

Tillage, animal husbandry, and construction do not ordinarily require the undivided attention of members of the production organization. It is quite possible to cultivate a field, tend a herd, or build a house and be doing something else at the same time. In fact, in tillage and animal husbandry, there are limits beyond which more exclusive attention paid to the process would in effect be wasted, since at some point there is no alternative but to wait for crops and animals to mature of their own accord. Similarly, in such processes, failure of one member of the production organization to perform his role correctly would not ordinarily result in immediate failure of the entire process.

In contrast, hunting and fishing ordinarily require that members performing the work not do anything else at the same time. Some search procedure is generally necessary, away from locations where other activities are carried on and specifically directed toward finding game or fish. Furthermore, once the quarry has been located, undivided attention is often necessary to keep it under control, since it is subject to random movement of its own accord. Success frequently depends on every member doing competently and effectively what he is supposed to do. In hunting by drive or surround, for example, failure of one or a few members on the job may result in the break-through and escape of the quarry.

These arguments imply the following propositions:

11. Hunting and fishing tend to be carried on by organizations emphasizing specificity; tillage, animal husbandry, and construction, by organizations emphasizing diffuseness.

	Specificity	Diffuseness
Hunting and fishing	28	24
Tillage, animal husbandry, and construction	8	67

$$Q = +.81 \qquad X^2 = 26.10 \qquad P < .001$$

12. *Hunting and fishing tend to be carried on by organizations emphasizing achievement; tillage, animal husbandry, and construction, by organizations emphasizing ascription.*

	Achievement	Ascription
Hunting and fishing	13	25
Tillage, animal husbandry, and construction	8	52

$$Q = +.54 \qquad X^2 = 4.84 \qquad P < .05$$

Furthermore:
13. *Organizations emphasizing achievement tend also to emphasize specificity.*

	Specificity	Diffuseness
Achievement	14	6
Ascription	23	68

$$Q = +.74 \qquad X^2 = 13.89 \qquad P < .001$$

Solidarity

The previous discussion of work load indicates that some organizations have institutionalized means of adding and subtracting members during the course of a process whereas others do not. Those members of a production organization who remain members from the beginning of the process until its completion will be referred to as the *basic* element of the organization. Persons who become members only in the performance of certain tasks and are not members at other times will be termed the *auxiliary* element. Not all organizations have auxiliary elements; those which do not will be termed *autonomous* organizations, while those which do will be referred to as *basic-auxiliary* organizations.[15]

A *permanent* production organization is defined as a production organization having a permanently assembled group as its basic element. Such a group may or may not be exclusively concerned with production; it need only be institutionalized as permanent. Thus in contemporary America both the modern industrial firm as well as the family carrying on agricultural production on a small farm constitute permanent production organizations. All other production organizations—those with nonpermanent basic elements —will be considered *temporary*.

It would appear reasonable that processes which require relatively long periods of time for their completion would be more likely to be carried on by permanent organizations than those of shorter duration. On the other hand, it is perfectly possible for short processes to be carried on by permanent organizations—only relatively less likely, because permanent relationships are less essential.

Thus:

14. *Tillage, construction, animal husbandry, and manufacturing tend to be carried on by permanent organizations; hunting, fishing, and collection, by temporary organizations.*

	Permanent	Temporary
Tillage, construction, animal husbandry, manufacturing	79	3
Hunting, fishing, collection	28	39

$$Q = +.94 \qquad X^2 = 51.54 \qquad P < .001$$

Similarly, a variable work load leaves open the possibility of basic-auxiliary organization, while a constant work load does not. Autonomy, however, can coexist with a variable work load, if the presence of all members is institutionalized during slack periods—a possibility which seems relatively unlikely. Hence:

15. *Tillage and construction tend to be carried on by basic-auxiliary organizations; hunting, fishing, and collection, by autonomous organizations.*

	Basic-auxiliary	Autonomous
Tillage and construction	38	22
Hunting, fishing, collection	5	61

$$Q = +.90 \qquad X^2 = 41.01 \qquad P < .001$$

Proprietorship

Proprietorship has already been defined as the right to control possession of outlay. For reasons of operational expediency, the discussion will refer largely to land and raw materials. Any individual or group enjoying rights of proprietorship will be referred to as a *proprietor*.

Three forms of proprietorship may be distinguished. Under *managerial* proprietorship, proprietary rights are vested in that manager (or those managers) in the topmost position(s) of authority in the organization. Under *corporate* proprietorship, such rights are vested in the organization as such, through some organizational mechanism in which all members participate in whatever way. *Separated* proprietorship, as the term implies, involves a situation wherein proprietary rights are vested neither in a manager nor in the corporate body, but in some individual or group independent of the production organization. Many writers have observed that societies practicing settled agriculture are relatively less likely to possess any kind of corporate property arrangements than are societies where agriculture is not practiced. Thurnwald, for example, argues that types of production which involve operations on rigidly fixed land areas with specific raw materials lend themselves more readily to personal (i.e., managerial or separated) forms of proprietorship than do processes which inherently involve diffuse land areas with raw materials of an essentially unpredictable character. For in the former type, relatively specific items of property are available for allocation which at the same time are sufficiently small in size that only a few persons are required to exploit and oversee them sufficiently to enforce rights of control. Corporate proprietorship is by no means precluded, but does not tend to be necessary, as in the case of vast land areas and highly diffuse raw materials.[16]

If this argument is correct, the following proposition would be expected to hold:

16. *Tillage and construction are associated with managerial or separated proprietorship; hunting, fishing, and collection, with corporate proprietorship.*

	Managerial or separated	Corporate
Tillage and construction	54	6
Hunting, fishing, collection	18	42

$$Q = +.90 \qquad X^2 = 42.53 \qquad P < .001$$

Recruitment

Although the study of recruitment is more directly pertinent to relationships between organization and social structure, technology nevertheless does set certain limits on recruitment possibilities. One may first of all classify recruitment patterns according to whether the selection criteria employed are predominantly *social* or *territorial*. Within each of these classes, different forms of obligation to participate may then be noted; this further breakdown will be discussed in Chapter Five.

Recruitment criteria are designated as *social* to the extent that membership is determined by prior or simultaneous membership in another organization. In contrast, recruitment criteria will be deemed *territorial* to the extent that membership may consist of anyone conveniently present and physically qualified, regardless of social affiliations.[17]

To the degree that marginal role performance is essential to a process, as is frequently the case in hunting, the question arises as to whether social recruitment criteria are adequate to ensure such performance. They may or may not be; at best, they are not likely to be particularly germane to effectiveness one way or the other. Thus one would expect the following proposition to hold, but with the possibility of many exceptions:

17. *Hunting organizations tend to be based on territorial recruitment; tillage and construction organizations, on social recruitment.*

	Territorial recruitment	Social recruitment
Hunting	19	12
Tillage, construction	5	54

$$Q = +.88 \qquad X^2 = 26.35 \qquad P < .001$$

As expected, a considerable number of hunting organizations are based on social recruitment, despite a general tendency to the contrary. The general relationship between achievement and territorial recruitment is apparent in the following proposition:

18. *Organizations in which rewards are distributed on the basis of achievement tend to be based on territorial recruitment.*

	Territorial recruitment	Social recruitment
Rewards based on achievement	14	8
Rewards not based on achievement	26	63

$$Q = +\,.61 \qquad X^2 = 7.36 \qquad P < .01$$

Exceptional Cases

A number of significant over-all relationships have been shown to exist between technology and organization. However, in many cases, a fairly large number of exceptions is apparent. Moreover, such exceptions often occur under quite different circumstances from what one would expect on purely technological grounds. Thus in proposition 11 one might well anticipate a considerable number of exceptional tillage, animal husbandry, and hunting organizations emphasizing specificity, inasmuch as that attribute is by no means technologically dysfunctional to these processes, but merely unnecessary to them. Actually, most of the exceptions take the form of diffuse hunting and fishing organizations. One would hardly expect this, since diffuseness is likely to be quite disruptive to hunting or fishing, with specificity tending to be essential. The same is true of proposition 12, where many exceptions quite unaccountably take the form of ascriptive hunting and fishing organizations. On the other hand, the exceptions to propositions 14 and 15 occur where one would expect them; there is no reason why hunting and fishing organizations could not be permanent, and tillage and construction organizations, autonomous. There is merely no technological reason why they would have to be. Proposition 16, however, returns to the original pattern. The exceptions appear in the "wrong" cell. From a technological standpoint, corporate proprietorship would be perfectly feasible in tillage and construction, but almost never occurs there in fact. On the other hand, despite the fact that managerial or separated proprietorship in hunting, fishing, or collection would be expected to be extremely difficult if not altogether impossible on technological grounds, it occurs there more than one-fourth of the time. And similarly, in proposition 17, the degree to which hunting is socially recruited seems inordinately high.

The structure of these exceptions may be taken as indicative of institutional pressures on organization structure, to the extent that tendencies run directly counter to what would appear necessary from a technological viewpoint. Thus they suggest the existence, under certain conditions, of strong social pressures toward diffuseness, ascription, managerial and separated proprietorship, and social recruitment in hunting and fishing, despite technological expectations to the contrary. Furthermore, such pressures, if they can be isolated, may well prove to be of some importance, inasmuch as most of the tendencies which they seem to produce are away from, rather than toward, "rational" administrative characteristics. On the other side of the ledger, propositions 14 and 15 indicate that many more permanent and autonomous organizations appear than would be necessary on purely technological grounds; institutionalization of these characteristics of modern administrative structure evidently presents fewer difficulties than might be supposed. That this may be a mixed blessing, however, is suggested by the following relationship:

19. *Specific organizations tend to be temporary; whereas diffuse organizations tend to be permanent.*

	Temporary	Permanent
Specific	34	17
Diffuse	7	90

$$Q = + .92 \qquad X^2 = 56.05 \qquad P < .001$$

Thus there is reason not only to suspect the existence of rather strong institutional pressures which can take precedence over technological considerations under certain conditions, but also to presume that they produce some significant tendencies away from "rational" administrative characteristics. Furthermore, it appears that the attribute of permanence, at least, is associated with certain of these "nonrational" characteristics.

The Structure of Production Organization

It is significant that, despite the exceptions just discussed, relationships between many of the internal structural characteristics of production organizations exhibit a remarkable degree of consistency. In other words, cases which are structurally inconsistent with technology in one respect tend to be inconsistent in other respects in such a way as to be structurally integrated internally. To recapitulate briefly, any production organization may be associational or bureaucratic; specific or diffuse; ascription-centered or achievement-centered; permanent or temporary; autonomous or basic-auxiliary; managerial, separated, or corporate as to proprietorship; and socially or territorially recruited.

Internal consistencies are the most striking with respect to the following four dimensions: specific vs. diffuse roles, permanent vs. temporary solidarity, autonomous vs. basic-auxiliary solidarity, and territorial vs. social recruitment. Out of sixteen logically possible combinations of these attributes, only four occur with any degree of regularity, accounting for over 90% of the cases; only seven combinations were ever observed at all, even when all 426 cases—all cases from every society—were counted. The resulting array (using the sample of 150 with data lacking in one instance) assumes a scale-type pattern, as Table VI indicates.

TABLE VI
INTERNAL CONSISTENCIES IN PRODUCTION
ORGANIZATION STRUCTURE

Temporary	Specific	Territorial	Autonomous	Total Organizations
34	34	34	34	34
7	..	..	7	7
..	15	15	15	15
..	2	..	..	2
..	..	4	4	4
..	..	..	40	40
..	..	..	..	47
			N =	149

The following propositions may thus be asserted:

20. *Temporary organizations tend to be specific, territorially recruited, and autonomous.*

	Specific, territorial, autonomous	Other
Temporary	34	7
Permanent	15	91

$$Q = +.93 \qquad X^2 = 59.87 \qquad P < .001$$

21. *Specific organizations tend to be territorially recruited and autonomous.*

	Territorial, autonomous	Other
Specific	49	2
Diffuse	4	92

$$Q = +.99 \qquad X^2 = 118.08 \qquad P < .001$$

22. *Territorially recruited organizations tend to be autonomous.*

	Autonomous	Basic-auxiliary
Territorial	53	0
Social	47	47

$$Q = +1.00 \qquad X^2 = 36.69 \qquad P < .001$$

23. *Basic-auxiliary organizations tend to be permanent, diffuse, and socially recruited.*

	Permanent, diffuse, social	Other
Basic-auxiliary	45	2
Autonomous	40	60

$$Q = +.94 \qquad X^2 = 38.48 \qquad P < .001$$

The positive association between specificity and territorial recruitment could be anticipated from structural-functional theory. Fairly reasonable sounding ex post facto explanations can be adduced to account for the other relationships. One must, however, guard against the persuasiveness of such explanations, precisely because such a variety of them are always so readily at hand. For example, it would appear quite awkward and unnecessary for temporary organizations to institutionalize auxiliary elements, precisely because the basic core would be only temporary. Similarly, in societies in which over-all role differentiation is not very ramified, there would appear to be little room for highly "specialized," specific organizations, territorially recruited, on a permanent basis. While these "persuasive explanations after the fact"—a phrase which Wilbert Moore is fond of using in this connection—may well have some grains of truth in them, the actual situation is much more complex, as will be shown in subsequent chapters. None of these relationships is true by definition, nor are the reasons for them quite so obvious as may appear on the surface.

On the basis of these findings, a provisional distinction may be made between four major types of nonindustrial production organization.

1. Temporary/specific/territorial/autonomous: 34 observed.
2. Permanent/specific/territorial/autonomous: 15 observed.
3. Permanent/diffuse/social/autonomous: 40 observed.
4. Permanent/diffuse/social/basic-auxiliary: 47 observed.

Types 1 and 2, with specificity and territorial recruitment, are those most closely akin to "rational" administrative organization.

Type 1, however, is temporary, while type 2 is permanent. The latter therefore bears the closest structural affinity to the modern Western industrial firm. In contrast, types 3 and 4 are more "traditional" than "rational." Although permanent, both types are characterized by diffuseness and social recruitment, and are thus rather far removed organizationally from Western industrialism.

The three other organizational dimensions are not quite so consistent in their interrelationships, although a number of significant associations occur:

24. Basic-auxiliary organizations tend to involve managerial or separated proprietorship.

	Managerial or separated proprietorship	Corporate proprietorship
Basic-auxiliary	44	3
Autonomous	45	48

$Q = +.87$ $X^2 = 25.66$ $P < .001$

25. Achievement tends to be emphasized in specific, territorially recruited, autonomous organizations.

	Specific, territorial, autonomous	Other
Achievement	14	8
Ascription	23	68

$Q = +.67$ $X^2 = 10.43$ $P < .01$

Thus organization type 2 exhibits a further tendency toward "rational" administration. With respect to proprietorship, however, this type does not particularly tend toward the norm of industrial capitalism:

26. *Among autonomous organizations, corporate proprietorship is associated with territorial recruitment.*

	Territorial	Social
Corporate	40	8
Managerial or separated	11	34

$$Q = +.87 \qquad X^2 = 30.18 \qquad P < .001$$

The association-bureaucracy dimension is not significantly related to any of the major organizational variables set forth here. As has been shown, however, it is closely related to technology, as are the other "rational" administrative characteristics of specificity, territorial recruitment, and emphasis on achievement. These latter three characteristics, though, are closely related to one another. Bureaucracy on the other hand does not seem to form part of the same system, but appears to occupy a different level of analysis altogether. The present findings would be consistent with the theory that bureaucracy depends on *amount* of attention as determined by over-all technological complexity, whereas a necessity for specificity, territorial recruitment, and an achievement emphasis derives from the *kind* of attention involved, irrespective of its amount. There is therefore no necessary reason for bureaucracy to be associated with these other three attributes or vice versa, unless appropriate similar amounts and kinds of attention happen to be combined in the same situation. It is thus quite misleading to consider bureaucracy as such to be an attribute of "rational" administrative systems per se; it appears to have nothing to do with the degree of rationality of action involved, aside from being a limiting factor with respect to gross effectiveness.[18] The practical significance of this finding is that the mere existence of large, ramified, bureaucratic production organizations in a nonindustrial society does not mean that that society possesses those organizational foundations essential to industrialism. On the contrary, it will be shown in a later chapter that, if anything, the opposite tends to be true.

Returning now to the earlier discussion of exceptional cases in light of these findings, it appears that the explanation of the presence of temporary "rational" organizations (type 1) on technological grounds is essentially correct, inasmuch as such organizations virtually never appear as exceptional cases. Arguing from a similar technological base, one would expect permanent "rational" organizations (type 2) to be very rare indeed, since from a technological standpoint they are generally unnecessary in nonindustrial contexts. One would also expect that, on those presumably rare occasions when they do appear, they would emerge as alternatives to their temporary counterparts, since permanence as such is in no way technologically disruptive; at worst, it is merely unnecessary. In light of the facts, these latter two arguments are unsound. Although type 2 organizations are the least common of the four types, they are far from being extremely rare. Furthermore, they are not associated with the same kinds of processes as are type 1 forms, but appear to be equally distributed over all technological conditions. In actual fact, permanent "traditional" organizations of type 3 appear as alternatives to type 1, and do so under technological conditions which seem quite inappropriate. On the other hand, permanent "traditional" organizations very often occur exactly where one would expect them to on technological grounds. Basic-auxiliary types (type 4) almost always do. And much of the time, type 3 appears as an alternative to type 4, as would be expected, since autonomy is technologically unnecessary rather than disruptive, under such circumstances.

Thus one is forced to regard technology with mixed feelings as a predictor of organizational structure. As a predictor of single, general tendencies, it fares quite well. In the area of authority structure, it fares extremely well indeed—much better, it is submitted, than has generally been supposed. However, in certain respects it is inadequate for explaining major variations, and in other respects it is downright misleading. Specifically, technology provides no clue as to when to expect autonomous as opposed to basic-auxiliary "traditional" organizations. Furthermore, it does not explain the surfeit of "traditional" type 3 forms under conditions where one would expect "rational" forms of type 1 or 2. Finally, technology tells us nothing about the rather curious distribution of permanent "rational" organizations (type 2). Recourse to institutional factors is necessary to cast light on these problems.

NOTES TO CHAPTER THREE

1. See Levy, *The Structure of Society, passim.*
2. Weber, *The Theory of Social and Economic Organization,* 152-3; K. Davis, *Human Society,* 94-5.

3. Adapted from Levy, *The Structure of Society*, 350-1. Only one of Levy's three dimensions of "solidarity" is employed here.

4. It is recognized that this definition departs considerably from standard usage, in that it is much broader. The purpose here is to avoid "ideal-type" rigidity, so as to be able to pose the question of the presence or absence of other "bureaucratic" attributes empirically.

5. W. E. Moore, course lectures in Industrial Sociology, Princeton University, 1955.

6. Graicunas, "Relationship in Organization," in Gulick and Urwick, *Papers in the Science of Administration*, 183-7.

7. Urwick, "Organization as a Technical Problem," in *ibid.*, 54; Hamilton, *The Soul and Body of an Army*, 229-30; DeJong, *Die Menselijke Factor in de Bedrijfshuishouding en de Bedrijfseconomische Problematiek*, 113; Kendall, "The Problem of the Chief Executive," *Bulletin of the Taylor Society*, VII, No. 2, 40; R. C. Davis, *The Influence of the Unit of Supervision and the Span of Executive Control on the Economy of Line Organization Structure*, 3; Dale, *Planning and Developing the Company Organization Structure*, 51. Indebtedness is also due to an unpublished paper by Arthur J. Kover, a graduate student at Yale University, entitled "Some Factors Affecting the Span of Control in Bureaucratic Organizations," (1957), and to personal conversations with Harrison C. White, of the Carnegie Institute of Technology.

8. For a replication arriving at the same conclusion with a different sample, see Udy, "The Structure of Authority in Nonindustrial Production Organizations," forthcoming in the *American Journal of Sociology*.

9. Weber, *Essays in Sociology*, 196 ff.; also see Blau, *Bureaucracy in Modern Society*, 28-33.

10. Taylor, *Shop Management*.

11. Maunier, *La construction collective de la maison en Kabylie*, esp. p. 65; Lowie, *Military Societies of the Crow Indians*; DuBois, *Monographie des Betsileo*, 434-40.

12. See Levy, *The Structure of Society*, 306-7.

13. Below, Chapter Six.

14. Levy, *op. cit.*, 248-62; Parsons and Shils, *Toward a General Theory of Action*, 80 ff.

15. Based on a combination of Weber's dichotomies: "autonomy-heteronomy," and "autocephaly-heterocephaly." See Weber, *The Theory of Social and Economic Organization*, 148.

16. Thurnwald, *Economics in Primitive Communities*.

17. Maine, *Lectures on the Early History of Institutions*.

18. For further discussion and justification of this position see Udy, "'Bureaucratic' Elements in Organizations," *American Sociological Review*, XXIII, 415-18.

4

ORGANIZATION STRUCTURE
AND SOCIETY

SOME OF THE LIMITS which technology places on organization structure do not appear to be particularly subject to cultural variation, in that very few exceptional cases seem to occur. However, those instances in which large numbers of exceptional cases are found suggest areas in which organization structure is subject to modification through social influences. In particular, a notably large number of hunting organizations turn out in fact to be diffuse, ascription-centered, permanent, socially recruited, and with managerial or separated proprietorship, despite technological expectations to the contrary. Similarly, there appear to be an unaccountably large number of autonomous tillage and construction organizations, despite the technological adequacy of basic-auxiliary forms for these processes. The ensuing discussion will attempt to identify the specific social conditions under which such exceptions may be expected.

Specific Forms of Recruitment

In analyzing the structure of any production system, recruitment is a crucial variable, since the process by which people become members of production organizations clearly has reference both to organizational as well as general social structure. Particularly important are the kinds of social affiliations already likely to be institutionalized between prospective members, since such affiliations are likely to be carried over into production and thus have a decided effect on organizational structure. The character of these affiliations depends on the recruitment criteria, the kind of group or aggregate from which members are drawn, and the nature of the obligation to participate.

The variation of recruitment criteria from social to territorial, and the concomitant variation of the source of membership from organized group to relatively unorganized aggregate, has already been discussed. The social-territorial dimension may further be broken down on the basis of the obligation to participate. Examination of the data in this light suggested five general types of recruitment: familial, custodial, contractual, reciprocal, and voluntary. The first two types are predominantly social in character, and the latter three, predominantly territorial.

Familial Recruitment

Recruitment is *familial* if the obligation to participate is based on ascribed kinship status. Personnel are drawn from some kind of kinship group, which may range in size from a nuclear family to a ramified set of extended kin relations. Membership is compulsory in the sense that sanctions of whatever sort relative to the maintenance of kinship solidarity are operative. Other institutional content may operate to reinforce kinship obligations, but need not consistently do so, and may be highly variable.

Production organizations recruited in this way tend to be permanent and diffuse, since, in effect, an established kinship group simply adds production to its already existing set of functions.

Custodial Recruitment

In *custodial* recruitment, the obligation to participate is based on differential ascribed power, with kinship status secondary, if operative at all. Personnel are drawn from some group defined in predominantly political terms. Membership is compulsory in that participation may be legitimately compelled by force, if necessary, or sanctioned by severe punishment. Again, additional reinforcing institutional content may or may not be present.

Essentially, custodial recruitment involves the translation of a set of prior sociopolitical affiliations into organizational terms, with the distinction between managers and workers institutionally determined on these grounds. The resulting production organization is almost always permanent and diffuse, since a set of permanent relationships relevant in a number of functional contexts is simply carried over into a production situation.

Contractual Recruitment

Contractual recruitment, as the name implies, is defined as determination of organizational membership by the conclusion, at some point, of a voluntary contract between two or more parties; i.e., an agreement to behave in a specified way for a specified time in the future.[1] Once the contract has been concluded, participation in accordance with its terms is generally considered compulsory, but with specific means of enforcement highly variable. The basis of recruitment tends to be territorial, inasmuch as there is no invariant social obligation to conclude any agreement in the first place. Social elements, however, do enter into contractual agreements, with organizational variations on this score generally assuming one of three possible forms. In the first type, the source of personnel is some relatively small group which is neither predominantly familial nor predominantly political in nature. It may be of any other kind—age-grade society, military society, general mutual aid association, or whatever. A voluntary contract is concluded between some proprietor on the one hand and this group or its legitimate representative on the other, by virtue of which the group then performs work for the proprietor —generally under its own management—with participation compulsory in terms of the agreement. In the second type, a number of individuals conclude an agreement to work together for some common productive interest. Participation is again compulsory in terms of the agreement, but methods of enforcement often appear quite weak. The third type is precisely like the second except that the agreement is between a number of separate individuals, on the one hand, and a manager-proprietor, on the other.

Most organizations recruited in this way are permanent, in that the agreement to work is set up in such a way that members can be replaced without altering the organization structure. Such is not always the case, however. Similarly, there is a strong tendency toward specificity, depending, however, on how explicit the agreement is. Contractual recruitment is subject to considerable variation in these respects, and is rather flexible.

Reciprocal Recruitment

Reciprocal recruitment, again as the name implies, is defined as the determination of membership on the basis of reciprocal obligations. A performs work for B in return for past or anticipated future work of a similar nature performed by B for A.

Participation is compulsory in that institutional sanctions of various kinds—in addition to the sanction of being unable to secure assistance in work—generally attach to nonparticipation. Reciprocal requirement is primarily based on community residence and propinquity, and is hence primarily territorial. Additional, social, criteria, however, notably kinship, are by no means infrequent. A considerable emphasis on achievement is involved, as is apparent. Measurement of work performed, however, is generally quite gross, but not always; sometimes rather ingenious precise methods are used.

An argument could be made for treating reciprocal recruitment as a special case of contractual recruitment. However, reciprocity seems to be based on general institutional expectations, rather than any special contractual agreement. Reciprocal recruitment appears to be used only for auxiliary elements; no organizations with basic elements recruited in this manner were observed.

Voluntary Recruitment

Voluntary recruitment is defined as determination of membership on the basis of self-defined self-interest, with no purely social sanctions attached to nonparticipation. This does not mean that severe personal deprivations cannot result from failure to participate, but only that no social mechanism is present which is expected to compel membership. Recruitment criteria are territorial, in the sense that anyone who can do the work and who happens to be in the vicinity may join. An expectation of achievement is usually involved; ability is either supposed to be self-evaluated, or is explicitly set up as a criterion for membership. Such achievement may be institutionalized in two different ways. In the first type, managers are self-appointed and select workers on the basis of demonstrated ability, with their capacity to secure workers correlatively dependent on the prospective workers' estimate of the manager's capabilities. In the second type, workers participate on their own assumption that they are able to do the work in question, and elect or acclaim a manager or managers on the basis of presumed superior ability.

Organizations recruited in this way are remarkably consistent as to structural characteristics. All are autonomous; all are temporary; and all are specific. Although such consistency does not obtain by definition, the reasons for it are hardly very astonishing.

Organizations formed this way are based on particular, single, common interests. If this interest is likely to be an enduring one, the probability of institutionalizing a specific permanent organization with no formal compulsion to participate seems virtually zero; under such circumstances, recruitment would almost certainly have to be on some firmer basis. By the same token, the degree of solidarity would appear so low that the capacity for recruitment of additional, auxiliary elements would seem virtually nil.

Institutional Types of Organization

The five forms of recruitment just described are differentially distributed over basic elements of autonomous organizations, basic elements of basic-auxiliary organizations, and auxiliary elements of basic-auxiliary organizations. Table VII shows this distribution.

TABLE VII

MODE OF RECRUITMENT OF OBSERVED
ORGANIZATION ELEMENTS

	Autonomous	Basic element of basic-auxiliary	Auxiliary element
Familial	11	44	6
Custodial	37	1	1
Contractual	21	2	13
Reciprocal	0	0	27
Voluntary	33	0	1
Unique	0	1	0

Production organizations may be classified by institutional type according to the form of recruitment of the basic element. Since reciprocal recruitment occurs only with auxiliary elements, this classification yields four major institutional types of production organization: familial, custodial, contractual, and voluntary. Subtypes may be derived on the basis of the autonomous vs. basic-auxiliary distinction, and on the basis of the form of recruitment of auxiliary elements. Table VIII gives the resultant typology, with all types observed enumerated, together with frequency of occurrence in the sample used for statistical purposes.

TABLE VIII
INSTITUTIONAL TYPES OF PRODUCTION ORGANIZATION

Major and Subtype	Freq. of Subtype	Freq. of Major Type
1. Familial	..	55
familial autonomous	11	..
familial-contractual	11	..
familial-reciprocal	27	..
familial-familial	6	..
2. Custodial	..	38
custodial autonomous	37	..
custodial-contractual	1	..
3. Contractual	..	23
contractual autonomous	21	..
contractual-any auxiliary	2	..
4. Voluntary	..	33
voluntary autonomous	33	..
Unique	..	1
Total		150

The various organizational types set forth in Chapter Three are not institutionalized at random, but are closely related to the four institutional types just discussed.

27. *Familial organizations tend to be basic-auxiliary, diffuse, and permanent.*

	Basic-auxiliary, diffuse, permanent	Other
Familial	44	11
Other	1	91

$$Q = +.99 \qquad X^2 = 97.23 \qquad P < .001$$

28. *Custodial organizations tend to be autonomous, diffuse, and permanent.*

	Autonomous, diffuse, permanent	Other
Custodial	29	8
Other	11	99

$$Q = +.94 \qquad X^2 = 61.95 \qquad P < .001$$

This distinction is not surprising in that basic familial elements are almost invariably smaller in size than basic custodial elements. This and the type of unit from which members are drawn constitute the two essential differences between these types. Seven of the eight custodial exceptions are temporary instead of permanent; the other is basic-auxiliary. The eleven exceptional familial cases are all autonomous.

29. *Contractual organizations tend to be autonomous, specific, and permanent.*

	Autonomous, specific, permanent	Other
Contractual	15	8
Other	0	124

$$Q = + 1.00 \qquad X^2 = 83.08 \qquad P < .001$$

Four of the exceptions are diffuse, but autonomous and permanent. The other four exhibit heterogeneous differences.

30. *Voluntary organizations tend to be autonomous, specific and temporary.*

	Autonomous, specific, temporary	Other
Voluntary	32	0
Other	2	113

$$Q = + .00 \qquad X^2 = 130.47 \qquad P < .001$$

Some of the above relationships are virtually true by definition. They are set forth explicitly to indicate the relatively small number of cases which do not fit the typology. Perhaps more revealing are certain relationships between institutional type and bureaucracy, achievement, and proprietorship of different kinds.

31. *Custodial organizations tend to be bureaucratic.*

	Bureaucracy	Association
Custodial	14	8
Other	18	38

$$Q = + .57 \qquad X^2 = 5.23 \qquad P < .05$$

32. *Contractual and voluntary organizations tend to emphasize achievement.*

	Achievement	Ascription
Contractual and voluntary	15	26
Other	8	64

$$Q = +.64 \qquad X^2 = 8.95 \qquad P < .01$$

33. *Custodial and familial organizations tend to involve managerial or separated proprietorship; contractual and voluntary organizations, corporate proprietorship.*

	Managerial or separated	Corporate
Custodial and familial	77	12
Contractual and voluntary	10	42

$$Q = +.92 \qquad X^2 = 60.07 \qquad P < .001$$

This set of relationships is rather disturbing. Not only is it consistent with the previous observation that bureaucracy is not particularly associated with "rational" administrative characteristics, but it goes on to suggest that some hiatus may be involved. For custodial organizations, which tend toward bureaucracy, epitomize the direct opposite of "rational" administration. Furthermore, an achievement emphasis, along with specificity, tends to be emphasized in institutional forms which do not tend to be bureaucratic. And managerial and separated proprietorship tend to occur largely in "nonrational" administrative forms.

Technology and Institutional Type

Similar difficulties are revealed in relationships between technological process and institutional type. In view of what has already been shown, the following proposition would be expected to hold:

34. *Tillage, construction, and animal husbandry tend to be carried on by custodial or familial organizations.*

	Custodial and familial	Other
Tillage, construction, animal husbandry	64	11
Other	29	46

$$Q = +.80 \qquad X^2 = 32.71 \qquad P < .001$$

It is thus apparent that the differences in use of custodial and familial forms revolve around the difference in use of autonomous or basic-auxiliary organizations. Basic-auxiliary forms are adequate to these processes from a technological standpoint, but apparently autonomous forms are frequently used nonetheless, and specifically where custodial organization is involved.

In view of earlier technological arguments, it would also be expected that hunting and fishing would be carried on either by voluntary or contractual organizations. It is true that:

35. *Hunting, fishing, and collection tend to be carried on by voluntary organizations.*

	Voluntary	Other
Hunting, fishing, collection	31	35
Other	2	82

$$Q = +.94 \qquad X^2 = 40.26 \qquad P < .001$$

None of these processes, however, appears under any conditions to be associated with contractual organization. On the contrary:

36. *If hunting and fishing are not carried on by voluntary organizations, they tend to be carried on by custodial organizations.*

	Custodial	Other except voluntary
Hunting and fishing	20	10
Other	18	69

$$Q = +.76 \qquad X^2 = 19.45 \qquad P < .001$$

Thus the key to the exceptions uncovered earlier appears to lie somehow in custodial organization. Pressures in the direction of custodial forms evidently result in an inordinate number of diffuse, ascription-centered, permanent hunting and fishing organizations with managerial and separated proprietorship. Similar pressures apparently result in autonomous, rather than basic-auxiliary, tillage and construction organizations. It remains, therefore, to identify the social sources of custodial organization, and the conditions under which it is likely to occur.

Institutional Type and Society

A *centralized government* will be defined as a concrete group having an ultimate monopoly on the legitimate use of force in a society of more than 1500 persons.[2] Custodial organization, by definition, must be based on some structure which at least resembles this, if it is to transcend other social affiliations. Similarly, it has been noted by other writers that the institution of contract implies the existence of some ultimate enforcing agency powerful enough to assure political stability.[3] These observations suggest the following proposition:

37. *Custodial and contractual organizations tend to exist only in societies having centralized governments.*

	Custodial and contractual	Other
Centralized government	42	27
No centralized government	17	53

$$Q = +.65 \qquad X^2 = 17.56 \qquad P < .001$$

The existence of centralized government thus suggests itself as a condition associated with the relatively high number of custodial organizations noted earlier:

38. *Under conditions of centralized government, hunting and fishing tend to be carried on by custodial, rather than voluntary, organizations.*

	Custodial	Voluntary
Centralized government	13	4
No centralized government	7	19

$$Q = +.79 \qquad X^2 = 8.24 \qquad P < .01$$

39. *Under conditions of centralized government, tillage, con-*

struction and animal husbandry tend to be carried on by custodial, rather than familial, organizations.

	Custodial	Familial
Centralized government	20	20
No centralized government	4	21

$$Q = +.68 \qquad X^2 = 6.24 \qquad P < .02$$

Contractual organizations cannot be shown to behave in the same way as do custodial forms under these conditions. While it is true that contractual organization is positively associated with centralized government, its over-all incidence is rather low. Furthermore, at no point in the analysis is contractual organization significantly associated with any particular type of process. If contractual are substituted for custodial organizations in propositions 38 and 39, the results are as follows:

	Centralized government	No centralized government
Contractual hunting and fishing	3	1
Voluntary hunting and fishing	4	19
Contractual tillage, construction, and animal husbandry	6	2
Familial tillage, construction, and animal husbandry	20	21

Frequencies are thus too low for meaningful analysis. It appears that, although centralized government tends to be a necessary condition for contractual organization, it does not in itself involve any mechanism which tends directly to further the development of contractual forms. Custodial organization, with its greater incidence and association with particular types of process, appears more dominant. Furthermore, custodial organization seems to occur even under circumstances for which it is ill-suited technologically. In this latter connection an important difference should be noted between the circumstances surrounding propositions 38 and 39.

Custodial organization is not technologically unsuited to any of the processes in proposition 39. Given propitious institutional circumstances, there is no technological reason why custodial forms should not occur in tillage, construction, or animal husbandry. Actually, table 39 suggests that custodial forms simply appear in addition to, rather than instead of, familial forms, in this context. Moreover, familial organization by no means tends to disappear under conditions of centralized government:

	Familial	Other
Centralized government	23	46
No centralized government	25	45

$$Q = -.05 \qquad X^2 = 0.01 \qquad P > .80$$

The situation regarding proposition 38 is notably different. As has been indicated, custodial organization, with its emphasis on diffuseness and ascription, is not well-suited technologically to hunting and fishing. Nevertheless, not only does it occur there, but under these conditions actually seems to appear instead of voluntary organization. For:

40. *Voluntary organization is negatively associated with centralized government.*

	Voluntary	Other
Centralized government	4	65
No centralized government	28	42

$$Q = -.83 \qquad X^2 = 21.04 \qquad P < .001$$

41. *If custodial organizations are present, voluntary organizations tend to be absent, in the same society.*

	Voluntary present	Voluntary absent
Custodial present	9	53
Custodial absent	30	25

$$Q = -.75 \qquad X^2 = 19.25 \qquad P < .001$$

Similar negative relationships do not hold between custodial and familial forms.

These findings indicate not only that custodial organization is widespread under conditions of centralized government, but that under this condition it tends to occur in all types of production, irrespective of its technological suitability, dominating contractual forms. At the same time, voluntary organizations tend to disappear, while familial forms remain, coexistent with custodial types. A mechanism which would explain this evidence is suggested by various theoretical writers and is further supported by other data in the present study. According to Linton, Herskovits, and others, centralized political authority tends ultimately to be based on a monopoly of control over outlay, particularly land.[4] In this connection a close dependence of centralized government on the practice of settled agriculture by a society may be noted:

42. *Societies with centralized governments tend to practice settled agriculture.*

	Agriculture	No agriculture
Centralized government	64	6
No centralized government	42	28

$$Q = +.75 \qquad X^2 = 17.13 \qquad P < .001$$

This relationship suggests that relatively stable, predictable land tenure arrangements are requisite to the development of a centralized political authority, although they do not guarantee such development. Furthermore, if control over outlay is important to the establishment of centralized government, the following proposition would be expected to hold:

43. *In societies with centralized government, production organizations are characterized by managerial or separated, rather than corporate, proprietorship.*

	Managerial and separated proprietorship	Corporate proprietorship
Centralized governmnet	49	14
No centralized government	26	38

$$Q = +.67 \qquad X^2 = 16.61 \qquad P < .001$$

Centralized government, therefore, involves a tendency toward central, diffuse control over resources. Custodial organization rests on role assignment on the basis of differential ascribed power, and also involves managerial and separated proprietorship. Consequently, under conditions of centralized government, custodial organization would tend to become generally diffused to all types of production, but particularly to those which involve outlay of rather large scope. As has been previously shown, hunting and fishing, as opposed to tillage, construction, or animal husbandry, fall in this latter category. Thus the facts uncovered here would be consistent with the theory that, when centralized government is introduced into a society, there is a tendency for all types of production to be carried out by custodial organization by virtue of pre-emption of control over resources by the political authority, particularly those which involve outlay which is large-scale and diffuse. Indeed it appears that this tendency is so strong in hunting and fishing that custodial forms actually replace voluntary ones. In tillage and construction, on the other hand, custodial forms seem to come into being in addition to rather than instead of familial forms, since the outlay involved is more specific and not so great in scope. Thus considerable evidence can be brought to bear on the theory that under conditions of centralized government, custodial organization tends to become generalized to all types of production by virtue of centralization of control over resources, and that this tendency will be stronger where resources are diffuse and broad in scope. Perhaps the most frequently discussed specific mechanism in this connection is the "conquest theory of the state," according to which the conquest of a settled agricultural people by a nomadic people generally results in expropriation by the latter of control over land and in the "specialization out" of a concrete political structure through which the conquerors maintain authority over the conquered. The result is a generalized political system maintaining ultimate control over possession of landed property, and on which custodial organization can potentially be based.[5]

The precise character of observed custodial organizations further indicates how this theory can be consistent with the differences discussed earlier between propositions 38 and 39. The practice of tillage under centralized government, for example, often involves the imposition of a custodial serfdom or peonage system on an already existing familial system. The latter continues to operate, while the former is utilized in support of the political establishment. In hunting, however, groups otherwise recruited voluntarily tend simply to be recruited by custodial *corvée,* inasmuch as no hunting areas are accessible to voluntary organizations having no control over land.

Although centralized government provides a context within which contractual organizations may ultimately develop, no direct mechanisms of the type just described appear to be involved. Contractual forms, being associated with corporate proprietorship, do not constitute part of the nexus of centralized control over resources. There is thus no institutional basis for their super-imposition on another type of system, or for their generalization to all types of production—despite their universal technological suitability. It is thus not surprising that many contractual organizations observed under these circumstances actually appear ancillary to over-all custodial structures. An example would be a contractual organization of serfs set up to manage irrigation facilities, in the context of a larger custodial framework. Furthermore, it can be shown directly that nonindustrial contractual, as opposed to custodial, forms do not tend to be generalized:

44. *Custodial organization is more likely to occur in more than one type of process in the same society than is contractual organization.*

	More than one type	One type only
Custodial	15	35
Contractual	1	31

$$Q = +.86 \qquad X^2 = 7.34 \qquad P < .01$$

It should be borne in mind here that, although government is often the actual concrete managerial agency involved in custodial organization, it need not be and frequently in fact is not; a variety of structures based on general social stratification may appear as perfectly adequate alternatives. All that is necessary is some structure which differentiates roles in terms of power and status; custodial organization per se does not imply "nationalized" production, as it were. Such structures, however, whether concretely part of the government or not, appear ultimately to be related to it in some way in that governments enjoy an ultimate monopoly on the legitimate use of force:

45. *Societies with centralized governments are more likely to possess complex hierarchies of general social stratification than are societies without centralized governments.*

	Complex stratification[6]	No complex stratification
Centralized government	56	11
No centralized government	23	44

$$Q = +.81 \qquad X^2 = 31.58 \qquad P < .001$$

Custodial organization, then, may actually be based on a non-governmental hierarchy of power, which in turn is ultimately sanctioned by governmental action. Certain types of peonage systems would be good examples of this, in which means of enforcing debt payments are ultimately sanctioned by force of government, and in which the wealthiest creditors often turn out to be government officials as well.

In view of the preceding discussion, it is readily appreciated why bureaucracy in and of itself does not necessarily imply "rational" administration, but may well imply just the opposite. For, as has been shown, custodial organizations tend to be bureaucratic; i.e., a pre-existing political hierarchy is imposed on a production situation. Such organization at the same time involves role assignment on the basis of ascribed political status, a de-emphasis of achievement as a standard for evaluating participation, and an emphasis on diffuse, rather than specific, objectives. Furthermore, organizations of this type appear likely actually to supplant former organizations of a more "rational" character, with specific objectives, territorial recruitment, and evaluation of role performance on the basis of achievement. Presumably this results in some decline in efficiency, since it often involves the use of organizational forms not technologically suited to the process at hand, particularly in hunting. Such a decline in efficiency is possible because it is accompanied by conditions which reduce the marginal importance of success in hunting and fishing. Centralized government is positively associated with the existence of settled agriculture. Thus, those conditions which tend to produce custodial forms in hunting and fishing at the same time tend to render these activities less important as sources of food supply.

One important implication of these findings is that nonindustrial societies with settled agriculture and centralized government are likely to be further removed administratively from industrialism than are more "primitive" societies. For voluntary organization has a closer structural affinity to modern industrial bureaucracy than do custodial forms. If the line of reasoning followed here is correct, one reaches the paradox that, in order for contractual organization of the type common in industry to develop at all, conditions must be present which in themselves tend to produce custodial forms instead, without contractual organization having much of a chance. And at the same time, it is presumably impossible for a number of reasons unrelated to the present discussion, such as the lack of a capital basis, to develop industry in societies of the type in which voluntary organization is likely to occur.

NOTES TO CHAPTER FOUR

1. K. Davis, *Human Society*, 470.
2. Levy, *The Structure of Society*, 485-6; Murdock, "World Ethnographic Sample," *American Anthropologist*, LIX, 674-86.
3. See W. E. Moore, *Economy and Society*, 29-30.
4. Linton, *The Study of Man*, 243-52; Herskovits, *The Economic Life of Primitive Peoples*, 372-87.
5. Davie, *The Evolution of War*, 160-75; also see Linton, *loc. cit.;* Herskovits, *loc. cit.;* Maine, *Lectures on the Early History of Institutions*, 64-97; Firth, *Elements of Social Organization*, 50-7.
6. *Complex stratification* is considered to be present where "three or more social classes or castes," or "hereditary aristocracy" is reported. Murdock, *op. cit.*, 673, 675-86.

5

INSTITUTIONAL MECHANISMS

MUCH OF A GENERAL NATURE has already been said regarding
the institutionalization of production. Each major institutional type,
however, involves certain peculiar problems which are not only
of some interest in themselves but also quite pertinent to the
study of reward systems. It seemed desirable, therefore, to devote
a separate chapter to the description of specific mechanisms involved in the institutionalization of each of the four major types.
The examples given below may be considered modal of the type
or subtype which they illustrate.

Familial Organizations

Familial organization, as has been shown, occurs most frequently in tillage, animal husbandry, and construction, and least
often in hunting and fishing. Its structure is always permanent.
In addition, it tends very strongly toward diffuseness and ascription, and is not particularly likely to be bureaucratic. Most familial
organizations are basic-auxiliary owing to the relatively small
size of the basic element; autonomous familial forms do occur,
however.

Autonomous and Basic-Auxiliary Types

The basic element of any familial organization is a residential
kin group of whatever type characteristic of the society in which
it is found. Despite the fact that residential kin groups may assume a wide variety of forms, all, from the viewpoint of production,
are quite limited in their possibilities owing to their relatively

small size. Furthermore, familial production organizations are, on the whole, fairly stable, and seem to be subject to much less variation in matters relevant to production than are the other three types. Consequently, no further subclassification of this type was deemed necessary.

The Tikopian household rarely consists of more than two nuclear families; two brothers, with their wives and children, may for example live together under one roof. This group often functions as a small production organization, frequently in an extremely simple manner. Husband and wife, for instance, may go fishing together. In tillage, the men and women work together in the household garden, with active direction in the hands of the household head. His wife and some of their children usually assist.

The Chagga household, on the other hand, is somewhat larger. Polygamy is common, and in addition several generations of the same lineage normally live under the same roof. Intergenerational assistance is institutionalized in tillage and dwelling construction, for example, with the parental generation forming the active core of direction.[1]

Such permanent basic familial elements are reported in almost every society studied. Autonomous organizations structured in these terms are too small and offer too few institutional problems to warrant special consideration. Basic-auxiliary familial organizations are of more interest. In this regard, basic familial elements are found combined with auxiliary contractual, reciprocal, and, to a lesser degree, further familial, elements.

Familial-Contractual Organizations

In familial-contractual organizations, auxiliary workers are added to the familial structure by virtue of a contractual agreement concluded between them and the family proprietor. It is agreed that they will aid the family in certain work for a certain time, and, generally, for specified compensation. There are two kinds of familial-contractual organizations, the "agency" type and the "individual" type.

In the "agency" type the proprietor concludes an agreement with another permanent organization, as a corporate group or with its legitimate representative, such that this organization in its entirety is recruited as the auxiliary element. The managerial structure of the auxiliary element is then imposed upon the entire system, and proprietorship becomes separated rather than managerial. Organizations which characteristically function corporately as auxiliaries may include, first of all, official governmental organizations. This form more properly involves a combination of custodial and contractual elements. Workers are recruited politically, and then put to work under an official to aid a family. A contractual agreement, however, between the family proprietor and the official is necessary before the group may be assembled.

> Among the Hopi, a working party could be arranged by anyone who had large fields to plant by application to the village and crier chiefs. The latter would announce the party four days in advance, and often the news would be relayed to other villages and a large number of persons would turn out. The proprietor was obliged to provide the noon and evening meals; much fun, gossip, and game-playing took place both during and after work.[2]

Another organization which may serve as an auxiliary is the guild. Guilds, essentially, are occupational groups having institutionalized monopolies on the performance of certain production activities. As such, they occur with some frequency as auxiliary elements in familial organizations. In most cases, however, it is not entirely clear whether the guild is properly an "agency" (i.e., whether the entire guild as a body acts as an auxiliary element) or whether membership in the guild is simply a requirement for individual employment in certain operations. Guilds, in some parts of Oceania, are the sole source of recruitment for certain experts in canoe and house building, at the stage of assembly and fitting in particular.

> Among the Tahitians and the Pukapukans, it seems clear that the canoe builders' guild definitely functions as an "agency" properly so-called. An agreement is concluded by which the expert and his assistants perform the work in return for food. In Buka culture, however, a "builder" is hired; men of certain families are renowned as experts and tend to form a "guild," which, however, appears to function mainly as a simple source of individual recruitment. In dwelling construction in Samoa, a master-builder may be called in; he brings his apprentices and associates with him and directs the work.[3]

The distinction between a genuine guild auxiliary agency and guild membership as a necessary qualification for individual wage work thus becomes blurred in many cases. Where sufficient data were available on authority and allocation, guilds were classed as agencies where proprietorship was separated.

The third category of organizations which characteristically function as auxiliary agencies is residual.

Among the Crow, the agency is a military or religious society. They functioned ". . . largely as mutual benefit organizations. If any one had to do a certain amount of work on his farm land, all his associates came to help him." Similarly, among the Zuni: "Assistance in the fields is obtained as follows: a member of a fraternity asks the *mosona* (director) for help, and he designates a certain member of the fraternity to assist their [sic] fellow."[4]

In other societies, age-grade associations based on mutual aid in performing bride-work function as auxiliary agencies.

Among the Dahomey, the *dokpwe* is a cooperative work organization composed of about 40-100 men. All able-bodied men are potential members, but the active core of membership consists of younger men who are cooperating in bride-work. The *dokpwe* may be summoned to aid in making a farm, roofing a house, or building a wall. Each *dokpwe* is headed by a chief (*dokpwega*), whose office is hereditary. Under him are three officers: the *asifaga*, who acts as general foreman in work projects; the *legede*, who sees to it that the members are present for work; and the *agutapa*, who makes announcements for the *dokpwega* at funerals, in connection with certain ceremonial functions of the *dokpwe*. These officials are chosen by the *dokpwega* from the young men of the village, with the advice and consent of the village chief. They hold office for life, unless they are remiss in the performance of their duties. In order to call upon the *dokpwe* for assistance in work, one must go to the *dokpwega* with a bottle of liquor, four yards of cloth, and two francs 50 centimes, which is divided between the *dokpwega* and the subchiefs. The *legede* is then instructed to notify the members to appear at the agreed time. The owner agrees to provide a meal of as rich and varied fare as possible, as compensation to the workers. As the work proceeds, "the *dokpwega*, carrying his staff of office, walks about, giving orders to his assistants to transmit to the men, while each of the subgroups names one of its members as headman and follows his orders, this being another instance of the rule that in Dahomey no group work is begun until a single responsible head is selected to direct it."[5]

Similar groups are found among the Hidatsa, Lobi, Tiv, Haitians (*combite*), and Nupe (*egbe*). The Iroquois possess an analogous women's mutual aid association. The Tiv *ihumbe* is similar to the Iroquois association; it involves a contractual agreement between household heads for mutual aid in tillage.[6]

In the "individual" type of familial-contractual organization, a contractual agreement is concluded between the family proprietor and individual persons to the effect that they will assist the familial group in work in return for agreed-upon compensation. This form seems particularly apt to occur in societies having some contact with Western industrialism. It is generally characterized by a setting of migrant agricultural workers, and often appears as a new mode of organization competitive with older familial-reciprocal forms.

> Among the Guatemalan peasants, kinship reciprocity prevails, but some men work for wages in the *milpas* of others. Telugu farmers employ migrant wage labor seasonally, drawn from migrant workers of the *Madiga* caste. Payment is in such cases in cash or kind; sometimes annual contracts are concluded. Similarly, among the Karen, tillage normally is carried on by the family, but extra women are sometimes hired to transplant rice shoots.[7]

Such cases are not necessarily limited to societies having contact with Western commercialism:

> Kwakiutl housebuilding was sometimes carried out by auxiliary wage workers. Similarly, among the Chukchee, members of poor families often hire themselves out to wealthy herdsmen for payment in kind.[8]

Foster presents an interesting and ingenious comparison of the relative efficiency of reciprocal and individual/contractual auxiliary labor in dwelling construction by the Popolucan Mexicans —a culture where both forms of work organization can be observed together. He concludes:

> "It thus appears that the system of voluntary communal [in our terminology, 'familial-reciprocal'] labor costs more than six times as much as hired [familial-contractual] help in efficient units. It becomes clear that this type of work is of a social rather than an economic nature. Units are too large for efficiency, and the atmosphere of good nature and fun causes each individual to work less intensively than he ordinarily would."[9]

Familial-Reciprocal Organizations

In familial-reciprocal organizations, the auxiliary element is recruited on the basis of institutionalized reciprocity. This type is not only extremely commonplace, but is surprisingly uniform in character from a comparative standpoint. Reciprocal recruitment was not observed other than in connection with auxiliary elements of this form.

There exist two basic kinds of familial-reciprocal organizations, which will be termed the *bolhon* and *palihog* types, respectively, using the Bisayan Filipino terms for them.[10] These forms are not mutually exclusive, and frequently even coexist side-by-side within the same type of production in a single culture. Unlike many of the other distinctions used here, the *bolhon-palihog* distinction is not exactly a "constructed type"; in a very real sense, it was "found." For, in a strikingly large number of instances, specific words were found for these two types in the native languages concerned; "*bolhon*" and "*palihog*" are accurately translatable directly into a number of languages of nonindustrial culture. The corresponding terms among the Maanyan, for example, are *hando* and *haweh*, respectively. The Saxon term for "*bolhon*" is *cyvar*. Such examples can be readily multiplied.

In the *bolhon* type, reciprocity occurs within a relatively small closed group of neighbors, engaged simultaneously in the same type of production, usually tillage. When auxiliary work is required, the group as a whole rotates from one proprietor to another, spending the same amount of time with each. The distinguishing features of the *bolhon* are that reciprocity occurs in rotation among the participants, with each participant serving as manager/proprietor in turn and receiving the same amount of work as measured by some relatively explicit standard, usually time or spatial area. All reciprocal obligations are thus automatically discharged in the course of a single complete "rotation."

> The Bisayan *bolhon* is used to work adjacent fields by neighbors, who are often but not necessarily relatives. One day is spent on each field; if the work is then unfinished, the group moves on to the next field anyhow. If the proprietor desires more time spent on his field, he must pay for it. In the Maanyan *hando* system, several families agree to work plots in rotation, spending one day per plot. The rotation cycle is repeated until all work is performed. A man may leave the *hando* whenever he has returned all services given him; work performed may be returned by the man himself, his son, or

his wife. Similarly, in the Saxon open-field system, the acre strips were plowed in this manner by the *cyvar*. Each person who owned a strip brought his ox and other equipment, and the strips were plowed in rotation.[11]

The *palihog* system appears to be more common than the *bolhon* type. Under *palihog* reciprocity, neighbors are simply called in to assist, with the understanding that such a request will be reciprocated at some future time. As opposed to the *bolhon*, the *palihog* is called by one single proprietor only, the amount of work to be done is diffuse, and the time and occasion for reciprocation indefinite, although reciprocation is definitely expected.

Among the Bisayan, a *palihog* is called by a family head to assist in doing a job which one family cannot do alone. It is most frequently used for the repair or construction of dwellings. Hart notes, as Foster cited earlier, that more people are usually present in a *palihog* than technologically necessary. He states that at least ten people usually came to set houseposts, and that they all were in each other's way constantly. He expresses the view that two men could have done the job with much more ease and dispatch. Among the Navaho, the individual ready to plant makes this known and people come to assist on the day he designates. A similar pattern obtains in Malekula. Among the Kikuyu, the field owner invites his friends three days in advance.[12]

Familial-Familial Organizations

Familial-familial organizations are based simply on extensions of the principles involved in familial autonomous organizations to the recruitment of auxiliary elements. Very few instances were found. However, such forms may be more common than the sample would indicate since it is rather difficult to distinguish them operationally from autonomous familial forms.

Custodial Organizations

All custodial organizations are essentially politically based. Considerable variation occurs among them, however, in the degree of economic reinforcement present in institutionalization. Six forms may be discerned: *corvées*, serfdom, tenancy, peonage, slavery, and total mobilization.

The Corvee

A *corvée* is an organization in which workers are subject to being summoned to labor by some official having legitimate but diffuse authority over them. Upon being summoned, the workers must move to and assemble at the site of production. *Corvées* may be of two types: "American" or "African."

"American" *corvées*, so-called because they appear to be especially common in North and South American cultures, are almost entirely political in nature, with little direct economic support. The official, by virtue of his powers of office alone, can recruit personnel to perform limited, fairly explicit duties, usually at certain times only. Participation on each separate occasion is not ordinarily mandatory, provided the individual participates on most such occasions.

> The San Blas Cuna government involved a series of elected officials specifically charged with certain communal enterprises. Several were charged with housebuilding; two were in charge of transporting half-completed canoes from the forest to the river; several were responsible for the administration of the communal farms; others supervised path maintenance; sometimes, special officials supervised maintenance of fish nets. "When any one of these officials is in charge, all men, including all other officials, are subordinate to him." Similarly, the Hopi possess work parties summoned by the village chiefs through the crier chiefs to do work of certain specified sorts for officials. The obligation to work is based on "traditional loyalty for the village officers, traditional pride in the village . . ."[13]

Despite their relative popularity in the Western Hemisphere, "American" type *corvées* are by no means restricted to America, but are of worldwide distribution, being also reported, for example, in such diverse localities as Western Tibet, Polynesia, ancient Germany, as well as Africa. And, although economic content is usually absent, religious reinforcement is often present, as the following example (from an African culture) illustrates:

> The Lobi political hierarchy includes a Chief of the Hunt, who is charged with directing hunting. The position appears to be largely hereditary; it is usually held by the Priest of the Earth. By divination, he determines the place and day for hunting, which he proclaims in the market; all are then supposed to assemble at the prescribed time.[14]

"African" *corvées,* which, as may be imagined, are especially common in (though not restricted to) Africa, involve a combination of political and economic elements. Diffuse authority of the official commanding the work manifestly derives, at least in great part, from his control over land, rather than simply from his official position. Furthermore, participation tends to be mandatory on each separate occasion, rather than merely most of the time, and is usually not restricted only to certain kinds of work, but can apply to anything.

> Theoretical ownership of all tribal land by the chief, involving tribute rights from the soil, including statute labor, is common among the Bantu-speaking tribes. In the Zulu tribe, for example, the young men between initiation and joining the army were specifically set apart for such service at the direction of the chief's council. Such services occur in tillage, animal husbandry, hunting, fishing, and a variety of other processes. No reciprocity is involved. Among the Sotho, for example, ". . . young men between initiation and marriage are considered as set apart for public service, and are expected to lead the flocks to graze without remuneration . . . and to fetch building materials from a distance." Also "they assemble every year to dig up and sow the fields appropriated for the personal maintenance of the chief and his first wife. The exact rights of the Bantu chief to agricultural labour may vary, of course, from tribe to tribe. . . . But I have not noted a single Bantu society in which authority was not formerly maintained by such a system, even if conditions have now been changed very much by the introduction of European methods of cultivation." Among the Bemba, *umusala* labor (*corvée* for the chief) involved messengers' rounding up twenty to thirty people from the entire district, who worked for the chief for about one week under the supervision of the chief himself or of some official.[15]

Religious reinforcement is often present; for example:

> In hunting, among the Sotho, the chief sets the occasion by consulting diviners. In fishing among the Thonga, "every male must answer the chief's summons to go to the shore," and must be blessed by a descendant of the family originally inhabiting the fishing site. Among the Bemba, the chief has a monopoly on knowledge of rain-making techniques in tillage.[16]

"African" type *corvées* are by no means restricted to Africa:

In New Guinea, the Wogeo *kokwal* (hereditary headman) receives labor tribute for about one day per week, in tillage, construction, and collection, upon his direct demand. Muong fishing is at times carried on by an "African" *corvée*. The *tha lang* (feudal lord having control over land use) decides the time. A retainer sounds a gong, and workers arrive carrying rafts; several are impressed to carry the lord's equipment as well. A gong signals the arrival of the *tha lang* at the fishing site, and stops sounding when he launches his raft. Others may then launch. Another stroke of the gong signals the throwing of the net by the lord; the others may now fish. Upon another sound of the gong, fishers dive in and drive fish into the nets. The gong then sounds to signal the end of fishing for the day. In the Trobriand Islands, hereditary control of the soil rests with the headman, who summons villagers to work in his own gardens as well as on plots used by others. He also generally has a monopoly on certain essential forms of garden magic. He may call a *corvée* for general work (*tamgogula*), for a specific task (*kabutu*), or for work in another village in cooperation with other chiefs (*lubalabisa.*)[17]

The coexistence of American with African type *corvées* within the same society appears entirely possible. Among the Bemba, for example, hunting *corvées* for the village headman appear to be of the American type; this official, appointed by the tribal chief, does not have theoretical ownership over the land, and participation on each unique occasion is not mandatory.[18] As we have seen, however, *corvées* for the chief himself, who enjoys theoretical ownership of all the land, are of the African type.

Virtually all *corvées* involve managerial proprietorship; the manager exercises ultimate legitimate control over land use. This does not necessarily mean that he "owns" the land, or even that he is using it for his own purposes at the time. In some instances he does "own" the land, but in others, especially those of the American type, a general communal right of use may exist, but with the manager making specific allocations and setting specific standards in work which he directs, by virtue of such allocations. This too constitutes managerial proprietorship, as that term has been defined here.

Corvées of either type involve movement of workers to the site of production. In the remaining permanent autonomous custodial forms, the assembled unit by and large remains dispersed spatially, but is centrally managed. When necessary, raw materials are physically moved around the system.

Serfdom

Under serfdom, participation in production is rendered obligatory by residence on land, the ultimate use of which is controlled by a landlord. By virtue of such residence, the serf is politically subject to the landlord, who exerts legitimate control over land use, and by whose authority production is organized. The serf may not dissolve the relationship without the acquiesence of the landlord, and, in "pure type" serfdom, the landlord may not in principle dispossess the serf without the latter's permission. In general, medieval European serfdom was, at least technically, of the "pure" variety; in Oriental systems, such "purity" is generally either totally absent, or suffused under a combination of serfdom and debt peonage such that the question of the right of the landlord to dispossess the serf would ordinarily refer to a purely hypothetical situation. Under such conditions, the line between serfdom and peonage is often blurred.[19]

It seems highly probable that African *corvées* and serfdom are likely to exist simultaneously as different elements of the same custodial system, for both are institutionalized directly on the basis of land tenure. Centralized management of dispersed agricultural production with serfdom would provide a constant potential source of labor for centralized concentrated production of other types, given diffuse political authority. This condition is evident in medieval England, Tibet, Persia, Kashmir, and to a lesser degree, on the Roman *latifundia* of the Imperial era. Such a tendency toward African *corvées* under serfdom would constitute a mechanism through which custodial organization becomes generalized from tillage to other types of production.

Serfdom may be more or less centralized. It is centralized to the extent that the landlords are themselves subject to some higher political authority who may legitimately requisition labor through them from their serfs. This condition seems to predominate in the Near and Far East. Serfdom is decentralized to the degree that the landlords are independent of such authority, as was predominantly true in Europe during the Dark Ages, and in some parts of the Orient, notably Afghanistan, where both types may be observed. In the course of history, the Roman *latifundia* not only fluctuated between these two extremes, but also varied in their relative emphasis on serfdom, as opposed to peonage, tenancy, and wage labor.

In the second century B.C. free wage labor was used on the Roman estates, but became hard to obtain, owing to the demands of state military service for manpower. Wars brought captive slaves, however, who were put to work as compulsory wage laborers and who, in principle, could buy their freedom. Such slaves were often even entrusted with supervisory positions. Discontent was rampant, however, with constant revolts and frequent collusion between slave supervisors and workers in "stalling" on the job. By the first century A.D. conditions had become so bad that various reforms were attempted on a fairly large scale. The compensation (*peculium*) of the slaves was increased; some were settled as serfs; in addition, free tenants were introduced. After the time of Augustus, the slowing down and ultimate cessation of foreign conquests resulted in cutting off the supply of slaves. Itinerant free wage laborers were employed, and there was a tendency for the free tenants to become serfs through peonage. Centralized leasing operations functioned in various ways, apparently, to centralize the entire system during the Imperial era.

Tibet provides an example of centralized serfdom, although peonage and tenancy are also found as custodial forms. The population, in a general sense, is allocated to land by the Dalai Lama, with tracts assigned to officials in lieu of salaries. Within these tracts serfdom is hereditary; relatives are punished if a serf absconds. The landlords are absolute masters and may also order [African type] *corvées*. Several estates may be centralized under one landlord, who is in turn subject to the Dalai Lama. According to Bell, five levels of authority exist in estates management. Each separate estate has an agent, who is directly responsible to the landlord for general management of the estate. Under the agent is at least one official called the *lang*, who collects tribute and settles disputes. Under each *lang* are several headmen (*gem-pos*), who coordinate work, and under each headman are approximately 50-100 serf households. The agent normally has a staff assistant, the *tso-pön*, who, among other things, is in charge of transporting goods and raw materials through the system while the members remain dispersed. In tribal Iran, less centralization is present. The peasant holding is the basis of the village. Certain areas are reserved by the landlord for his own exploitation through African type *corvées*, and peasant holdings are allocated by him on the basis of the amount of land which can be cultivated by a yoke of oxen. It appears that occasionally the state could succeed in requisitioning labor from local landlords for work on state lands, depending on how powerful the central government happened to be at the time.[20]

Tenancy

In tenancy, economic aspects are still more in evidence than in the preceding forms, relative to political aspects. Nominally, an agreement is concluded between peasant and landlord concerning the way the produce of the land is to be divided between them. This agreement serves as the basis for participation in the organization, but differs from a contract in that the relative political position of the parties not only tends to set the terms of the agreement in advance, but renders some such agreement virtually mandatory. The length of time the agreement is to run therefore becomes indefinite; it is to all intents and purposes a mandatory agreement with an ultimately political basis.

There may exist pressures for tenancy, over time, to become transformed into serfdom via peonage. Political authority operates here in such a way that tenants tend to be forced irretrievably into indebtedness to the landlord. If such indebtedness is hereditary, and land tenure is also hereditary, the ultimate result is serfdom. The example of the Imperial Roman *latifundia* in this connection has already been cited. Furthermore, in the Tibetan and Iranian examples, indebtedness to the landlord seems to be present alongside of serfdom, particularly in the form of oppressive taxation. In Tibet, loans at 20-35 percent interest are also reported.[21]

It would seem, therefore, that tenancy in "pure" form may be unstable, in that it presupposes a more or less egalitarian relationship between landlord and tenant. When tenancy occurs as a subtype of custodial organization, such a relationship is by definition absent. By this token, one might suppose that tenancy in "pure" form could exist in a stable condition as a subtype of contractual, rather than custodial, organization. It is interesting, however, that tenancy arrangements never appear in the sample as a possible form of contractual organization. It would seem that tenancy tends to occur only under custodial conditions, and that because of this fact and by virtue of the diffuse political character of custodial forms, pressures are always present for tenancy to change into serfdom or peonage.

Repeated historical examples of such pressures are found in the history of the Roman *latifundia*. Attempts to settle free tenants on the estates after the first century A.D. were offset by centralized political control of the means of production through a system of fiefs and benefices. Borrowing or leasing was therefore necessary on the part of the tenants in order for them to carry on their daily work. Ultimately this led to serfdom via an intermediate stage of peonage. By the time of the fall of the Western Empire, the position of the once-free *coloni* was for all practical purposes one of serfdom, thus forming a basis for medieval European feudalism.

Dollard cites evidence from the present-day United States which suggests that tenancy tends to be incompatible with conditions propitious to the development of contractual forms, owing to its being bound up with the operation of the "subsistence theory of wages." In "Southerntown," it was possible to settle Negro tenants on farms only by keeping returns to the tenants so low that geographical mobility was financially impossible, in the face of an actual shortage of farm labor. The caste structure was such (and probably still is such) that this policy could be followed by political means. Thus tenancy emerges in "Southerntown" as an essentially custodial phenomenon and is characterized, for all practical purposes, by strong tendencies toward peonage and even serfdom.[22]

Peonage

Under peonage, economic pressures on the worker operate in a still more direct way. Differential political power is directly reinforced by economic indebtedness on the part of the worker to the manager. The worker may not leave the manager's employ until the debt is paid off; this is the essence of peonage. Interest, sometimes as high as 200% compounded annually, is generally charged such that the debt, for all practical purposes, can never be paid. The fact that such debts tend to be hereditary under peonage systems gives reason to believe that, when it occurs in tillage, peonage may tend to become transformed into serfdom over time. Tendencies are noted, for example, among the Thai, for persons to sell themselves into serfdom in order to pay their debts, with such indebtedness also serving as a basis for required participation in an African type *corvée*.[23]

The peonage system in pearling among the Maritime Arabs constitutes what might be termed a classic example. "It is difficult for one totally unfamiliar with the Arab East to understand the economic system of the Arabs. The tenets of Islam prevent any banking system, interest, usury, or insurance. The economy of the Arabs is built on a tremendous pyramid of debt which has the lowly sailor, fisherman, farmer, and coolie on the base, and a sheikh on top; this system, which may well be called the 'debt system,' operates efficiently and effectively, but has been notoriously overworked in the case of pearling activities in the Persian Gulf.

"At the start, a merchant will finance a *nakhoda* for building a deep-water dhow. Thus the *nakhoda* is the nominal owner of the dhow, but he is indebted to the merchant. If the *nakhoda* had enough money to buy a dhow himself, he would finance someone else and become a merchant himself. This arrangement suits the merchants, for if the ship goes down, the *nakhoda* (or his family) must pay back the value of the cargo and the cost of the dhow as well. Thus the merchant has an 'insurance' on his investment. A merchant may have a dozen *nakhodas* so indebted to him.

"The *nakhoda*, on the other hand, has all the sailors and crew indebted to him. He never pays them any regular wages, but gives them advances of food and money when they need it. . . . Only when the voyage has terminated six months or a year later, and the ship has been beached in the home port, do the sailors get their share of the earnings of the voyage. But by this time many of them have no share coming, as the *nakhoda* usually has advanced them more than their share amounts to, so he must give them another advance; this is to the *nakhoda's* liking, as he then has the sailors indebted to him. Once a sailor owes a *nakhoda* money, the sailor cannot ship with another *nakhoda* until the debt is paid."[24]

Whereas serfdom and tenancy are largely restricted to tillage, peonage is reported for both tillage and fishing. It is often intimately connected with the capital equipment frequently essential to the latter. Unlike the custodial forms previously discussed, peonage is likely to involve separated proprietorship instead of managerial proprietorship, by virtue of absentee landlordism. In Oriental culture, such peonage is a frequent adjunct to serfdom.

Slavery

American and African *corvées*, serfdom, tenancy, and peonage constitute the principal forms of permanent custodial production organization. A word or two needs to be said about the institution of slavery, together with reasons why it does not occupy a more prominent part in the discussion. Slavery is essentially a form of relationship wherein people are consistently treated as chattels.[25] Clear cases where "slaves" are not at the same time either serfs, peons, or wage laborers seem in fact to be rare. Thus slavery emerges as an extreme form of interpersonal relationship characteristic of serfdom or peonage, or as a condition of low wages combined with prohibited geographical mobility; the latter almost always involves serfdom. Slavery, as a basis of production organization, does not seem to be involved in the institutionalization of production independently of the above three forms.

Total Mobilization

A sixth form of custodial organization which may be either permanent or temporary, and which will be treated as a special case, is the mobilization of the total society, through a generalized political system, relative to a specific production objective. Present examples are limited to Oceania and the Plains Indians. These cases have been reported as diffuse, inasmuch as the relationships concerned are politically general; a specific orientation of the temporary type, in Plains buffalo hunting, could be cogently argued, however.

Total mobilization under a permanent political system is characteristic of certain large-scale fishing fleet operations in Oceania. Among the Mangaians, after a calm, everyone regularly assembled on the beach with canoes. The Hereditary Ruler of Food then took charge of the assemblage and conducted a magical ceremony to keep rough weather from arising. The men would then take their canoes into the open sea to fish; each canoe was under the direction of a *makona* (fishing expert) who was likely to be a family head and who usually passed his expert knowledge concerning weather signs and likely fishing sites on to his son. The Ruler of Food generally remained ashore and observed the weather signs. If a change was indicated, he signaled the boats to return, standing at the mouth of the lagoon and "checking off" [sic] the canoes one by one as they returned to be greeted on the beach by the women and children.

Among the Plains Indians, total mobilization under a temporary political system regularly occurred in connection with buffalo hunting. Among the Crow ". . . there was no strong central power except at the time of a buffalo hunt or of some similar occasion calling for concerted effort." Every year the principal chief, elected for the occasion, appointed a military society to serve as a police force to maintain order during the buffalo hunt, whose every act, however, he could veto if he saw fit. Three methods of hunting were used: surround, impounding, and driving over a cliff. In the surround method, scouts would disperse in a semicircle, perhaps twenty miles long, and move the herd in the direction of the village.

Couriers would be sent on ahead to warn the others, including the older men, women, and children, of the approach. Those at the village would form a line to block the herd. The scouts would then drive the herd against this group, who would kill the buffalo. Upon a signal from the chief, the rest of the herd was allowed to escape.[26]

From the above examples, one can see how custodial organization is based essentially on the political system, with economic and religious considerations entering in varying degrees. Under organized agriculture, the probable development of *corvées* out of serfdom or peonage in tillage provides a possible mechanism through which custodial forms tend to be generalized, through ascriptive recruitment, to other types of production.

Auxiliary Forms

Very few cases of custodial basic forms used with auxiliaries were noted. In each instance, the auxiliary element was recruited contractually, involving wage labor as an addition to the usual force. The case of the Roman *latifundia,* already cited, would be an example, where migrant wage workers were often used seasonally in peak periods, at certain times in Roman history.

Contractual Organizations

Contractual organizations may assume two basic forms: the agency type and the managerial proprietorship type.

Agencies

Where communal cultivation of land occurs, contractual agencies officially attached to the government, and recruited in the same manner as the auxiliary of similar type already described, appear likely to occur. This form differs from a *corvée* in that the members agree to be bound by the rules of the organization, and in a context of a somewhat narrower range of possible organizational functions. The structure, moreover, is set apart from the rest of the political system, and tends to be functionally specific as to tillage.

Guilds may also function as contractual organizations. Their contractual status is often marginal, however, in that ascriptive criteria frequently limit membership. Moreover, as in the case where guilds appear as auxiliary forms, it is often difficult to determine whether the guild functions as a production organization as here defined, or whether it exists as a sort of "professional association," with members working individually. Guilds seem particularly likely to occur in manufacturing, but are reported also for hunting and animal husbandry.

> Among the Nupe, guilds occur in metalworking, glass manufacture, weaving, bead-work, carpentry, and butchering. Each guild has a chief, and each separate shop a leader, who directs cooperation, supplies tools and raw material to hired auxiliary wage workers, and distributes proceeds among the guild members.[27]

The most common type of agency functioning as a contractual organization may be termed the Burmese *in* type, in which a number of persons agree to cooperate as a production organization to further a common interest. This form is always autonomous, but often bears a strong affinity to the *bolhon* auxiliary. It would not be unrealistic to place these two forms in the same category, except that the *bolhon* specifically involves reciprocity and is not consistently based on a contractual-type agreement. Furthermore, the familial-*bolhon* form quite consistently occurs under managerial proprietorship; the autonomous Burmese *in* type occurs under corporate proprietorship.

> Burmese *in* fishing involves a trap in the river which must be rebuilt every year, at an annual cost of 500-1000 Rs., and requiring the work of twenty men for about a month. Eighty to one hundred fishermen work at the one reported for six months out of the year. The fish are gathered up in baskets day and night by watches on a rotating basis, in shifts of eight or nine men at one time. The fish are kept alive and sent to market. Each member contributes an equivalent amount of money and work. The money is used to pay the government for fishing and auctioning rights, and for materials to construct the trap. At the end of the season, profits are equally divided, accounts having been kept of fish caught and sold. Four or five elders are in charge, who supervise, collect money, buy equipment, and keep accounts. Among the Ifugao, irrigation works are built and maintained in a similar fashion. A number of men whose fields need irrigation purchase an interest in a ditch, and build and maintain it together.

The Chiru *làm* is a contractual agency of from five to

eight families who agree to cooperate in the cultivation of communal village land. Each member family provides its own tools. The families are co-villagers, usually friends and neighbors. In Indo-China, with the demise of the *corvée*, villagers have in recent years tended to form such organizations for the upkeep of public property.[28]

The Managerial Proprietorship Type

The contractual organization with managerial proprietorship is familiar in modern Western culture. It is the type form of the American owner-managed small business. A proprietor simply hires a number of persons to work for him in return for wages in money or kind. The system is similar to auxiliary recruitment on an individual contract basis, except that the workers, here, are not auxiliary to a family. They, together with the manager/proprietor, form a permanent, specific, production organization.

> An alternative to Burmese *in* fishing, for example, is for a proprietor owning a fish trap to act as manager and hire men to work for him, operating the trap in return for wages.[29]

Auxiliaries

Each of the two contractual-auxiliary organizations reported is unique. Like other basic-auxiliary forms, however, both involve recruitment of labor for temporary assistance under peak work loads.

Voluntary Organizations

Voluntary organizations fall into three classes. In the first type, a given leader recruits, with admission to membership depending largely on competence; in the second type, a leader is elected or acclaimed by the participants on the basis of ability; and in the third type, participation is largely undifferentiated or casual, but with a valuation on success.

Leader-recruited Types

Recruitment by a given leader frequently occurs when a hunter of recognized superior ability appoints himself leader and seeks followers:

Among the Sanpoil, anyone could theoretically organize a hunt, "but in each community certain men were reputed to be good hunting leaders and usually only these instigated trips. Others would have found it difficult to get followers." Preparations for the trip, starting time, and deployment of the force were subject to the leader's direction. He selected men for each post, according to whether they were good shots or good runners.[30]

Sometimes, leadership is based on a minimal degree of ascription:

Among the Gilyak, in order to organize or direct a seal-hunting expedition, one must first own a boat. However, within the boat, labor is divided specifically between the harpooner, the oarsmen, and the helmsman. The owner (*pilang*) acts as helmsman if able; if not, someone else does. The best oarsmen are placed toward the stern. The best shot is placed forward.[31]

Leader-elected Types

Election or acclamation of a leader on the basis of competence may be direct or he may hold office by virtue of previous appointment to another position made on the same basis.

Among the Northern Paiute, the chief directed hunting, but was acclaimed chief on the basis of hunting skill. Others were renowned especially for skill in antelope charming.[32]

In some cases, such leaders are elected permanently (but with tenure contingent on skill) and a state of constant readiness is institutionalized such that when game or fish are sighted, assembly and activation is immediate:

Among the Aleut, whaling was carried on under the direction of chosen chiefs (*toyones*). Certain men ascend bluffs to try to spot whale schools. Upon sighting a school, they give a signal. Immediately the "best men" start out in boats. In each boat, one man, who is a good marksman, spears; the other paddles. The former is in charge. The boats deploy, with coordination by standard signals. When the whale is harpooned, it dives. The boats return, and sentinels are ranged on the bluffs to spy for the carcass when it comes to the surface, about three days later. The dead whale is then hauled ashore.[33]

Casual Types

Undifferentiated participation frequently occurs in the form of mass efforts when sheer strength of numbers is required. Individual achievement is relatively less in evidence, although gross success is valued.

> Among the Azande, when elephants are sighted, "all the people of the neighborhood are called." Thousands are gathered together by signals on wooden drums. Everyone capable of bearing arms participates. Fires are lit on all sides and the animals move toward the center. Spears are thrown from behind the fires. Sometimes, elephants are driven into an area where they can be speared from trees.[34]

Participation in collective fish-poisoning is often quite casual; frequently recreational functions quite apart from production objectives are evident. Gillin says, for example, of this activity among the Caribs, that it was characteristically "a sort of picnic or field day."[35]

Problems of Institutionalization

One of the most striking distinctive features of collective production is the possibility of hiatus between technology and culture. In an ongoing production system, this usually assumes the form of certain technological patterns which are latent in the sense that they are initially unforeseen but subsequently must be recognized. The possibility always exists that such patterns may not be readily institutionalized, or, in extreme cases, that they may even run counter to culturally prescribed behavior. Such problems, which are created by inadequate institutionalization, may be cognitive or motivational in nature.

In this context, *cognition* refers to the perception of the organization structure by its members, in particular of division of labor. The problem here is one of differentiating the requisite number of roles. For example, any process involving four specialized operations at some point ordinarily requires that at least seven roles be differentiated in the organization performing it: one corresponding to each operation plus three more which differentiate levels of authority. Furthermore, these latter three roles must be capable of being differentiated on an hierarchical basis. The recruitment structure may be such that this division of labor is already present in the affiliations of members prior to their commitment to production. If so, institutionalization will be adequate from a cognitive standpoint. There is, however, no guarantee that such will be the case. It is somewhat more likely under conditions of social, as opposed to territorial, recruitment, since the former manifestly involves pre-existent social relationships among prospective members. Thus in the case of familial and custodial organization, existing kinship and political differentiation may be adequate to distinguish the requisite number of roles in the manner required. In the case of contractual and voluntary forms, the problem is potentially more acute, for "external" bases of role differentiation are less likely to be directly operative. In either case, however, there is no guarantee of adequate cognition on the basis of already institutionalized relationships among members.

Motivation, here defined simply as the institutionalization of effort, presents a similar problem. Inasmuch as every production organization is dependent upon its social setting for members, these members will possess varied personal goals which do not necessarily correspond to organizational objectives. There is no reason to suppose, from a technological viewpoint, that organizational behavior will constitute an appropriate means for the realization of such goals. To the extent that it does not, the organization in question will face the problem of adequate motivation.[36] Again, this problem would appear likely to be less severe under conditions of social recruitment. Contractual and voluntary forms directly face the problem of rendering organizational objectives coincident with personal goals. In familial and custodial organization, however, productive labor is one part of a diffuse package of kinship or political obligations, as the case may be. This diffuseness broadens the potential scope of consequences of organizational behavior from the standpoint of the individual member, and thus increases the range of motivational possibilities in the situation. From another point of view, however, the disadvantages of such organizational forms derive precisely from this diffuseness. The type of orientation produced is not likely to be specifically directed toward production. Organizational roles are effectively linked to personal goals, but organizational mission is not. Thus from a motivational viewpoint, effective coordination of organizational activities is manifestly irrelevant. The possible consequences of this situation for over-all efficiency and effectiveness, therefore, are not too encouraging. Motivation is still likely to remain a problem, albeit in somewhat different form; namely, inefficiency.

Thus despite the institutional type of organization, and the nature of the obligation to participate, institutionalization of collective production is likely to involve problems of adequate cognition and motivation. Evidence will be adduced in the next chapter in support of the hypothesis that reward systems are oriented to the function of securing adequate cognition and motivation, and that their variations can at least in part be accounted for through independently observable differences in the cognitive and motivational structure of production situations.

NOTES TO CHAPTER FIVE

1. Firth, *We the Tikopia*, 100 ff.; Gutmann, *Das Recht der Dschagga*, 395; Raum, *Chaga Childhood*, 180, 210.

2. Beaglehole, *Notes on Hopi Economic Life*, 29.

3. Ivens, *The Island Builders of the Pacific*, 48-50; Forde, *Habitat, Economy, and Society*, 215; Ivens, *Melanesians of the South-east Solomon Islands*, 149-54; Mead, *Cooperation and Competition among Primitive Peoples*, 289.

4. Lowie, *The Crow Indians*, 208; Stevenson, *The Zuni Indians*, 350.

5. Herskovits, *Dahomey*, 63-77.

6. G. L. Wilson, *Agriculture of the Hidatsa Indians*, passim; Labouret, *Les tribus du rameau Lobi*, 144, 264-6; Downes, *The Tiv Tribe*, 25; Herskovits, *Life in a Haitian Valley;* Nadel, *A Black Byzantium*, 248-51; Quain, "The Iroquois," in Mead, *op. cit.*, 250-1; Lyford, *Iroquois Crafts*, 15; Abraham, *The Tiv People*, 212.

7. Wagley, *Economics of a Guatemalan Village*, 75; Dube, *Indian Village*, 78-9; H. I. Marshall, *The Karen People of Burma*, 76.

8. Goldman, "The Kwakiutl of Vancouver Island," in Mead, *op. cit.*, 180-209; Bogoras, *The Chukchee*, 83.

9. Foster, *A Primitive Mexican Economy*, 34.

10. See Hart, *Barrio Caticugan*, 431-3. In English, if one wishes, these types could accurately be termed "rotational reciprocity" and "discrete reciprocity," respectively.

11. Hart, *loc. cit.;* Provinse, "Cooperative Ricefield Cultivation among the Siang Dyaks of Central Borneo," *American Anthropologist* XXXIX, 77-102; Seebohm, *The English Village Community*, 117-25.

12. Hart, *loc. cit.;* Hill, *The Agricultural and Hunting Methods of the Navaho Indians*, 28; Deacon, *Malekula*, 182-5; Kenyatta, *Facing Mount Kenya*, 55-60.

13. Stout, "The Cuna," in Smithsonian Institution, *Handbook of South American Indians*, IV, 261; Beaglehole, *op. cit.*, 29.

14. Labouret, *op. cit.*, 122-4.

15. Richards, *Hunger and Work in a Savage Tribe*, 146; Casalis, *Les*

Bassoutos, 162, 266; Junod, *The Life of a South African Tribe*, I, 406.
16. Casalis, *op. cit.*, 179-80; Junod, *op. cit.*, II, 85-8; Richards, *loc. cit.*
17. Forde, *op. cit.*, 299; Cuisinier, *Les Muong*, 176; Malinowski, *Argonauts of the Western Pacific*, 156-63; *Coral Gardens and their Magic*, 157 ff.
18. Richards, *Land, Labour, and Diet in Northern Rhodesia*, 342-50.
19. In this connection it is pertinent to point out that the historical origin of medieval European serfdom has often been traced to military exigencies arising from political disruption following the breakup of the Roman Empire. Oriental serfdom, on the other hand, has been held to have developed to a significant degree out of peonage combined with hereditary indebtedness. See Maine, *Village Communities in the East and West;* Wittfogel, *Oriental Despotism.*
20. Cary, *A History of Rome*, 259-60, 451-2, 561-2, 666 ff.; Heitland, *Agricola*, 151 ff.; Pelham, *Essays on Roman History*, 300 ff.; Shen and Liu, *Tibet and the Tibetans*, 103; Rockhill, *Notes on the Ethnology of Tibet*, 680; MacDonald, *The Land of the Lama*, 123; Kawaguchi, *Three Years in Tibet*, 429; Bell, *The People of Tibet*, 302; Lambton, *Landlord and Peasant in Persia*, 4-7, 120.
21. S. C. Das, *Journey to Lhasa and Central Tibet*, 120. Dollard reports similar interest rates charged tenants in "Southerntown" U.S.A. in *Caste and Class in a Southern Town*, 110.
22. Cary; Pelham; Heitland; *loc. cit.;* also see Boissonade, *Life and Work in Medieval Europe*, first part, *passim;* Dollard, *op. cit.*, 108 ff.
23. Young, *The Kingdom of the Yellow Robe*, 126.
24. Bowen, "The Dhow Sailor," *American Neptune*, IX, 193-4. Cf. Dollard, *loc. cit.*
25. See Nieboer, *Slavery as an Industrial System.*
26. Te Rangi Hiroa, *Mangaian Society*, 145-7; Lowie, *The Religion of the Crow Indians*, 357-9.
27. Nadel, *op. cit.*, 256 ff.
28. Orr, *Field Notes on the Burmese Standard of Living*, 14-18; Goldman, "The Ifugao of the Phillipine Islands," in Mead, *op. cit.*, 153-79; J. C. Das, "Some Notes on the Economic and Agricultural Life of a Little Known Tribe on the Eastern Frontier of India," *Anthropos*, XXXII, 446-9; Goudal, *Labour Conditions in Indo-China*, 28.
29. Orr, *op. cit.*, 16.
30. Ray, *The Sanpoil and Nespelem*, 77-82.
31. Kreinovich, "Morskoi promysel giliakov derevni Kul'," *Sovetskaia Etnografiia*, 1934, No. 5, 78-96.
32. Kelly, *Ethnography of the Surprise Valley Paiute*, 182-3; Lowie, *Notes on Shoshonean Ethnography*, 304.
33. Elliott, *Our Arctic Province*, 248-9, 152-3; Collins, *The Islands and Their People*, 28-9; Veniaminov, *Zapiski ob ostrovakh Unalashskinskago otdela*, 342 ff.

34. Lagae, *Les Azande ou Niam-Niam*, 147-9; Schweinfurth, *The Heart of Africa*, 438; Brock, "Some Notes on the Zande Tribe . . .," *Sudan Notes and Records*, I, 256.

35. Gillin, *The Barama River Caribs of British Guiana*, 11-12.

36. W. E. Moore, *Industrial Relations and the Social Order*, 263-4; Simmel, *The Web of Group Affiliations*.

6

REWARD SYSTEMS

As DEFINED EARLIER, a reward is any material object which accrues to an individual as an institutionalized consequence of participation in a production organization, and a *reward system*, that pattern of allocation of rewards among members. Any reward system involves: 1) the rewards themselves, 2) the parties to whom allocations are made, 3) allocative mechanisms, and 4) allocation criteria. Every production organization possesses some kind of reward system, if only because the product made must be allocated to some party, through some mechanism, according to some set of criteria, given the universality of property systems.

Produce—the sum total of products made—is therefore by definition universally present as a reward. In addition, money and/or goods in kind may or may not be present. *Money*, as here used, refers to any generalized medium of exchange manifestly recognized as such. *Goods in kind* comprise all material objects which are neither produce nor money.

Any reward system may involve allocations of the above rewards to managers, workers, or both. Allocation to management will be referred to as *leiturgical;* allocation to workers, as *compensatory*.[1]

Leiturgical or compensatory reward allocation occurs through the mechanisms of accumulation or distribution. By *accumulation* is meant accrual to a party solely as a result of a transformation of raw materials, without any transfer of rights of possession taking place. Of the three items mentioned above, therefore, only produce can accumulate since accrual of money or goods in kind requires some transfer of possession rights. Furthermore, all reward systems by definition involve accumulation of produce. Such accumulation may be either leiturgical or compensatory. *Distribution* is defined as accrual resulting from a transfer of rights of possession from one party to another. Thus distribution may take place of produce, money, goods in kind, or some combination of these, and may be either leiturgical or compensatory. However, distribution may or may not be present in any given reward system; some are characterized by accumulation only. Reward systems involving both accumulation and distribution, as well as both leiturgical and compensatory allocation, will be said to be *balanced*. All other forms of reward systems will be termed *unbalanced*. Unbalanced systems therefore may involve accumulation only, or they may involve both accumulation and distribution but consistently of a leiturgical or compensatory sort. In addition, entire reward systems may be classified as "leiturgical" or "compensatory," depending on the party to whom the last allocation is made.

It is thus possible to distinguish four basic types of reward systems. In a *balanced compensatory* reward system accumulation of produce to management is followed by distribution of rewards (produce, money, and/or goods in kind) to the workers by management. In a *balanced leiturgical* reward system produce accumulates to the workers who then distribute produce, money, and/or goods in kind to management. An *unbalanced compensatory* reward system involves accumulation of produce to workers with no distribution of rewards to management; and an *unbalanced leiturgical* reward system, accumulation of produce to management with no distribution of rewards to workers.

Regardless of the point at which allocation is made, the party to whom it is made, or the mechanism involved, institutional criteria must be present as a basis for such allocation. Five such criteria seem to be of especially frequent occurrence cross-culturally: *proprietorship, gross participation* (whether or not the member is present and participating, without reference to finer gradations of performance), *achievement* (differential performance), *organization office,* and *status ascribed independently* of the production organization.

At the outset it was hypothesized that the structure of any reward system is determined partly by the nature of the production organization and partly by the social setting within which it exists, within limits set by technology. This working hypothesis will now be examined, first, in its relationship to technology, and secondly, as it relates to organization and social setting through the problems of cognition and motivation, as set forth in the preceding chapter.

Technology and Rewards

Technology sets limits on reward systems in certain ways, some of which are fairly obvious and others of which are rather subtle. It has already been shown that hunting tends to involve distribution of rewards on some basis of achievement, in the presence of a high marginal importance of role performance by any single participant. Other technological limitations on rewards are perhaps less subtle, but deserve mention as setting limits on the possible effects of organizational and institutional influences in this area.

In the first place, some types of process are of such a nature technically that accumulation of produce to workers is a physical impossibility. Where this is the case, the only forms of reward system possible are balanced compensatory or unbalanced leiturgical. Certain kinds of construction and most forms of manufacturing are quite obvious examples. Relatively complex forms of hunting tend to be similar. In tillage, furthermore, the fact that crops ripen at times likely to be independent of any work currently going on makes worker accumulation of produce difficult. Consequently, the following proposition holds:

46. *Tillage, hunting, construction, and manufacturing tend to be characterized by balanced compensatory or unbalanced leiturgical reward systems, while fishing, collection, and animal husbandry tend to be characterized relatively by unbalanced compensatory or balanced leiturgical reward systems.*

	Balanced compensatory or unbalanced leiturgical	Unbalanced compensatory or balanced leiturgical
Tillage, hunting, construction, and manufacturing	67	11
Fishing, collection, and animal husbandry	25	16

$$Q = +.59 \qquad X^2 = 8.14 \qquad P < .01$$

In tillage and construction, furthermore, the product is of such a nature that it cannot easily be distributed. Persons assisting in planting, for instance, in tillage cannot receive part of the crop. And manifest "distribution" of use of a constructed object would seem likely to involve fairly complicated institutionalization. Therefore:

47. *In balanced reward systems goods in kind are more likely to be distributed in tillage and construction; produce, in hunting, fishing, and collection.*

	Goods in kind	Produce
Tillage and construction	31	6
Hunting, fishing, and collection	0	32

$$Q = +1.00 \qquad X^2 = 45.35 \qquad P < .001$$

Apart from the above fairly obvious propositions, further limitations on reward systems of a technological nature are not evident.

Reward System, Organization, and Institutionalization

Within these technological limits, reward systems are determined both by organizational and general social structure in the sense that they appear to be functionally oriented to the solution of problems of institutionalizing certain organizational features under certain social conditions. As indicated earlier, problems which reward systems appear to solve, in stable production systems, center on the questions of adequate motivation and cognition. From a motivational standpoint, participation in any production organization may be analyzed as resulting from some combination of three institutionalized conditions: obligation to participate, sanctions against nonparticipation, and rewards. The relative strength of each of these factors varies according to the organizational and institutional situation. For present purposes, it will be postulated that participation in production requires a certain amount of motivation; that all such motivation derives from these three sources; and consequently that lack of "force" from one source must be compensated for by increased "force" from one or both of the other two sources. Motivation alone, however, is not enough. Given sufficient motivation to participate, the member must also be able to identify the way he is supposed to participate, from a cognitive point of view. This is a simple matter where division of labor in the production organization is based on some general societal mode of role differentiation. An example would be a production organization with two positions differentiated in the structure of division of labor, one of which is performed by men, the other by women, under conditions of general societal role differentiation on the basis of sex. In situations of this kind, the prospective member can easily determine what he is supposed to do. In a more complex division of labor, however, as for example much specialization combined with a high degree of bureaucracy, it is possible that the criteria provided by general societal role differentiation will prove insufficient to discriminate all of the positions differentiated by division of labor. Under such circumstances, the necessary additional amount of finer discrimination can be secured by attaching differential rewards to the positions. The occupational structure of modern industry perhaps provides the most striking example of complex role differentiation on the basis of differential rewards, under frequent extreme conditions of "loss of public identity of the job."

In the above terms, four general functions of reward systems could be discerned: 1) assurance of adequate recruitment, 2) maintenance of an adequate level of performance, 3) integration of the authority structure, and 4) assurance of adequate role differentiation.

The second function has already been discussed; hunting tends to involve differential rewards on the basis of achievement, inasmuch as adequate role performance tends to be crucial to success of the process. This function, as well as the first and third, tends to relate to motivation; the fourth, to cognition. Different types of reward systems will now be discussed in this context, as they apply to the institutionalization of various organizational features.

Balanced and Unbalanced Systems

Only in balanced reward systems do reward items flow through the authority structure. Distribution proceeds either from higher to lower or lower to higher authority, depending on whether the system is compensatory or leiturgical, respectively. Only systems of this type, then, are capable of integrating authority structure or of differentiating roles on the basis of authority. It seems reasonable to suppose, then, that the greater the number of levels of authority, the more severe these problems are likely to be. Therefore:

48. Bureaucracies tend to possess balanced reward systems; associations, unbalanced reward systems.

	Balanced	Unbalanced
Bureaucracy	23	3
Association	22	15

$$Q = + .67 \qquad X^2 = 4.95 \qquad P < .05$$

Balanced Compensatory and Unbalanced Leiturgical Systems

The most common forms of reward systems are balanced compensatory and unbalanced leiturgical. A comparison between them is useful because the former proves to be characteristic of organizations where the obligation to participate is not strongly institutionalized, and the latter, where it is. In voluntary and contractual recruitment, the obligation to participate is not automatically prescribed socially, but depends on some agreement; furthermore, nonparticipation is not ordinarily very strongly sanctioned.

49. Voluntary organizations and organizations with basic or auxiliary contractual elements tend to possess balanced compensatory reward systems.

	Balanced compensatory	Other
Voluntary or with contractual elements	44	10
Other	38	27

$$Q = + .51 \qquad X^2 = 6.26 \qquad P < .02$$

In such organizations, the workers are compensated by management for their participation, with minimal sanctions and relatively less social obligation to participate than in other types. The way is also open to an integration of authority structure, and a closer delineation of roles, since the resulting system is balanced. In contrast, some organizations are institutionalized on the basis of a very strong obligation to participate and/or rather severe sanctions against refusal. Familial-reciprocal organizations tend to be of the former type, since institutionalized reciprocity is involved. Custodial *corvées* tend to be of the latter type. Obligation to participate is often very strongly institutionalized, at least in ideal, hortatory terms, and in any case is usually sanctioned by the use of force. Thus it may be said that:

50. *Familial-reciprocal organizations and custodial* corvées *tend to be characterized by unbalanced leiturgical reward systems.*[2]

	Unbalanced leiturgical	Other
Familial-reciprocal and custodial *corvées*	18	49
Other	1	53

$$Q = +.90 \qquad X^2 = 12.30 \qquad P < .001$$

There are a number of exceptions to the above proposition; most such exceptions are balanced compensatory. It has been seen that in *bolhon* type familial-reciprocal organizations, close track is generally kept of reciprocal obligations, with a specific mechanism frequently present which automatically insures reciprocity. In *palihog* types, however, reciprocity obligations are likely to be considerably more flexible and diffuse. Therefore:

51. Bolhon *type organizations tend to involve unbalanced leiturgical systems relative to* palihog *types, which are relatively more likely to involve balanced compensatory systems.*[3]

	Unbalanced leiturgical	Balanced compensatory
Bolhon	9	10
Palihog	6	30

$$Q = +.63 \qquad X^2 = 4.46 \qquad P < .05$$

Thus again, where obligation to participate is relatively weak, and sanctions not severe, balanced compensatory reward systems tend to be used. Apparently, in most societies, as in our own, people will work without compensation only where they feel very strongly that they ought to or where they can be forced to do so.

Balanced Leiturgical Systems

This type of reward system appears to be characteristic only of certain kinds of custodial organizations; namely, serfdom, tenancy, and peonage. In such organizations, units carrying on production are typically scattered, accumulating produce themselves, all or a portion of which is handed over to management. Sanctions are ordinarily strong enough to avoid the necessity of worker compensation, and leiturgical contributions emerge as being closely connected with the authority structure in the form of a means of control over widely diversified holdings. Bureaucracy is also frequently present, with differential rewards by office.

52. *Serfdom, tenancy, and peonage tend toward balanced leiturgical reward systems.*

	Balanced leiturgical	Other
Serfdom, tenancy, and peonage	18	1
Other	7	95

$$Q = +.99 \qquad X^2 = 70.18 \qquad P < .001$$

Unbalanced Compensatory Systems

This form is in a sense a special case, and occurs where "organization" is rather marginal. For workers simply accumulate produce either with no allocation to management as such, or with allocation to those people who are managers occurring in a context external to the production organization. In either of these cases, the question arises as to whether the unit analyzed ought really to have been classified as a "production organization." For role differentiation is already institutionally given, little discernible authority structure peculiar to production is evident, and obligations to participate tend to be obligations to associate with the group involved rather than specifically to engage in production. In the sample here, such marginal cases most frequently take the form of familial autonomous organizations, where members of the same family may well simply happen to be working together.

53. *Familial autonomous organizations tend to be characterized by unbalanced compensatory reward systems.*

	Unbalanced compensatory	Other
Familial autonomous	22	7
Other	10	80

$$Q = +.92 \qquad X^2 = 43.59 \qquad P < .001$$

In view of these findings, it may be possible to maintain that production organizations with unbalanced reward systems are potentially unstable.[4] Those with unbalanced compensatory systems are certainly marginal as production organizations. And those with unbalanced leiturgical systems seem to require so much institutional involvement as a structural substitute for compensation that they may prove to be subject to rather extreme pressures toward emphasis of functions other than production. Thus the recreational, "socializing" function of familial-reciprocal forms is often alluded to in the ethnographic literature.[5] And *corvées* appear frequently to be enmeshed rather strongly in the political system. This suggests that a clear "specialization out" of economic structure in a society tends to occur only in terms of organizations which are voluntary, involve contractual elements of some kind, or are based on serfdom, tenancy, or peonage. Other forms of organization seem to be of at least questionable reliability, insofar as "specialized" production is concerned.

Reward Items

As has been indicated, only produce, goods in kind, and money will be here considered to be reward items. It would be interesting to consider other possible items, such as prestige or esteem, but adequate comparative data are lacking.

The question of the type of item characteristic of unbalanced systems may be easily disposed of. Inasmuch as only produce can accumulate, the following two propositions are true by definition:

54. *In an unbalanced leiturgical reward system, rewards consist solely of produce, which accumulates to management.*

55. *In an unbalanced compensatory reward system, rewards consist solely of produce, which accumulates to the workers.*

Balanced systems have more ramifications. Produce accumulates and is "balanced" by a distribution of goods in kind, money, or part of the accumulated produce. The question therefore arises as to what kinds of items are distributed in balanced systems. Earlier it was shown that certain types of processes necessarily tend to emphasize certain distribution items. Given these findings, plus already demonstrated relationships between process type and institutional type of organization, the following relationships may be stated:

56. *In custodial or voluntary organizations with balanced systems, produce tends to be used as a distribution item, rather than money or goods in kind.*

	Produce	Other
Custodial or voluntary	33	6
Other	13	36

$$Q = +.87 \qquad X^2 = 27.08 \qquad P < .001$$

No significant differences were observed in this respect between compensatory and leiturgical systems.

57. *In familial organizations with balanced systems, money or goods in kind tend to be used as distribution items, rather than produce.*

	Money or kind	Produce
Familial	27	7
Other	15	39

$$Q = +.81 \qquad X^2 = 20.27 \qquad P < .001$$

These relationships are not surprising in that voluntary organizations, as has been shown, tend to carry on hunting and fishing, as do many custodial forms. Also, serfdom, tenancy, and peonage systems at times involve distribution of produce with tillage, once a year, at harvest. Familial organizations, on the other hand, tend to be associated with tillage or construction under circumstances where imposed once-a-year distributions are impossible.

A further relationship between contractual recruitment and money as a reward item is evident in the data:

58. *In balanced systems involving either basic or auxiliary contractual elements in the organization, money tends to be used as a distribution item.*

	Money	Other
Contractual elements present	18	17
No contractual elements present	5	77

$$Q = +.88 \qquad X^2 = 29.10 \qquad P < .001$$

This proposition applies to contractual, custodial-contractual, and familial-contractual structures, and may well be indicative of a positive relationship between the existence of a general medium of exchange and the incidence of contractual organization. Unfortunately, this possibility could not be explored using present data.

Allocation Criteria

Proprietorship is rather crucial in the allocation of rewards:

59. *Except in the case of familial autonomous organizations, some ultimate allocation of some item always occurs on the basis of proprietorship.*

With the exception noted, this proposition holds true of all cases studied. Two further propositions follow logically:

60. *Except for familial autonomous types, organizations with managerial proprietorship always involve accumulation or distribution to management.*

61. *Organizations with corporate proprietorship always involve accumulation or distribution to the workers.*

Familial autonomous organizations, as has been argued, constitute a marginal case. Many of them involve managerial proprietorship, but apparently with unbalanced compensatory rewards. Subsequent distribution along some lines, however, seems inevitable, if not in the context of the production situation itself.

Thus some allocation of produce on the basis of proprietorship is universal, apart from a very few scattered unique instances which are so unusual that they may be safely omitted from a general discussion. This implies that unbalanced leiturgical systems can occur only under conditions of managerial or separated proprietorship combined with a process which does not involve accumulation to workers, technologically speaking. Similarly, unbalanced compensatory systems can occur only under conditions of corporate proprietorship combined with a process which does involve accumulation to workers from a technological standpoint, apart from the already-noted familial autonomous exceptions. Departures from these two "ideal types," then, could result either from hiatus between technology and proprietorship, or institutional inadequacy of an unbalanced reward system, or some combination of these two conditions. The gross existence of balanced leiturgical forms with managerial or separated proprietorship, then, can be adequately explained on the basis of hiatus between technology and proprietorship: produce accumulates to workers under existing technological conditions, yet with managerial or separated proprietorship requiring some distribution of produce to managers. Balanced compensatory forms with corporate proprietorship can be similarly explained: produce accumulates centrally, yet under conditions of corporate proprietorship which require some distribution to workers. It is quite true that these types of reward systems, under these conditions, can and do perform other functions as well—indeed this has been shown to be the case—but, given the postulate that some allocation must occur on the basis of proprietorship, the purely mechanical character of the system alone is adequate to explain why the reward system has to be of the particular type in question and can assume no other form.

On the other hand, the existence of balanced leiturgical reward systems under conditions of corporate proprietorship, and balanced compensatory reward systems under managerial and separated proprietorship, must be explained wholly on the other grounds previously suggested. The former type is very rare, but the latter is extremely common. The tabulation below gives the frequency of occurrence in the sample:

	Managerial or separated	Corporate
Unbalanced leiturgical	9	1
Balanced leiturgical	7	0
Balanced compensatory	52	29
Unbalanced compensatory	7	10

Other allocation criteria appear largely as criteria of distribution of rewards, rather than accumulation. In cases where they are reported as accumulation criteria, they are virtually always combined with proprietorship such that separation is difficult. Therefore they will be discussed here mainly as they relate to distribution.

Gross participation (i.e., the state of being simply present and working) is of course in a sense always present as a reward criterion. It becomes important only in situations where it is the sole basis of reward allocation apart from proprietorship. One would expect this to obtain in situations where institutionalization of roles is quite clear, where performance motivation is not particularly important, but where simple recruitment tends to be a problem. This would seem to be the case where reciprocal recruitment occurs in the absence of sufficiently strong institutional obligations to admit of an unbalanced reward system. Hence:

62. *Among organizations where rewards are distributed, familial-reciprocal forms tend to be characterized by distribution on the basis of gross participation only.*

	Gross participation only	Other
Familial-reciprocal	12	5
Other	23	53

$$Q = +.69 \qquad X^2 = 7.98 \qquad P < .01$$

Reward allocation on the basis of achievement (differential performance) has been previously discussed, and has been shown to be characteristic of voluntary and contractual organizations. The question here is whether achievement is present in any respect; it is always accompanied by gross participation, by definition. Proprietorship is of course always present as well at some point. The characteristic reward item employed here is of some interest. Discrimination of different levels of achievement presumably requires some calibration, to which money is peculiarly suited. Goods in kind, or produce, can be calibrated, but apparently only with somewhat greater difficulty. Therefore it is not surprising to find that:

63. *Rewards based on achievement tend to consist of money; rewards based on other criteria tend to consist of produce or goods in kind.*

	Money used	Money not used
Achievement criteria used	14	29
Achievement criteria not used	2	67

$$Q = +.88 \qquad X^2 = 16.68 \qquad P < .001$$

Organization office and externally ascribed status are difficult to isolate as separate allocation criteria, independently of proprietorship. It has previously been shown that bureaucracies tend to involve situations where members holding different offices receive different rewards. Much of the time, however, differences in degree of proprietary control are also involved; by definition, "managerial proprietorship" implies a unity of the two. However, where many levels of authority are involved, and particularly where specialists are employed who have no proprietary interests, there appears to be some presumptive evidence of differential reward allocation on the basis of office independently of proprietorship. In any event, even where manifest justification of differences is made on the basis of proprietorship, a *de facto* difference by office also occurs.

The nature of reward differentiation by office, however, is not so clear as one might suspect. The following proposition holds true of all relevant cases where data were clear:

64. *In custodial and voluntary bureaucracies with rewards differentiated by office, the greater the amount of authority attached to the office, the greater the amount of the reward.*

The variables in the above proposition are relatively easy to observe, under the circumstances indicated, even in the absence of a general medium of exchange, since in custodial and voluntary organizations only one reward item—produce—is usually involved. In contractual and familial organizations, however, the situation is less clear. More than one reward item is usually present. In the absence of a generalized exchange medium, it is thus at best difficult to compare the relative "worth" of unlike items. Frequently the manager-proprietor receives produce, for example, and the workers, goods in kind, with comparison difficult between the two units. It is certainly not universally true that managers seek to give "less" than they receive under such circumstances. In many cultures, the giving of a feast following a work party is viewed as a means of gaining social prestige through showing generosity. There is again some presumptive evidence that where contractual relationships are involved, those in higher authority tend to get more, where similar units are involved. Thus, in contractual auxiliaries of the "agency" type, the Dahomean *dokpwega* and the Haitian *chef d'esquade,* both of whom are managerial officials but not proprietors, receive more of the same compensation than do the workers.[6] It is difficult to say whether they consistently receive more or less than does the proprietor, however, for the reasons discussed above.

Where specialists are involved, mention is often made of special compensation for them. The mason and carpenter in Kabyle dwelling construction, for example, have special portions of food reserved for them.[7] Examples of this sort could be multiplied, but not in sufficient number to permit generalization.

Exchange and Status

W. E. Moore has pointed out that monetary rewards tend to function as "universal means," especially in an industrial system, where media of exchange are highly generalized.[8] Reward systems in nonindustrial production do not in general have this characteristic, although where money is used, there is at least some tendency in this direction.

In all instances where money occurs as a reward, it is reported as exchangeable for at least some goods in kind. In addition, the following types of exchange possibilities were noted, from the point of view of the party receiving the reward concerned:

	Clear cases
Produce for goods in kind	2
Produce for money	16
Produce for general status	14
Goods in kind for money	1
Money for general status	1

It should be pointed out here, however, that no attempt was made to achieve a detailed general survey of relationships between economic and other institutions in any society studied. The data are therefore quite incomplete. Money is undoubtedly exchangeable for general status in a number of instances. However, it may be suggested that the other figures may reflect relative emphasis fairly accurately. Possession of produce may involve enhanced status. If such produce cannot be exchanged for money, however, it is more likely to be consumed than bartered. Goods in kind of the type used generally as compensation for work do not lend themselves to exchange, consisting as they usually do of food which will spoil if it is not immediately consumed.

General status appears to enter the work picture in two different ways, apart from its previously discussed role assignment function. In the first place, status may in some cases clearly be enhanced by possession of produce. Secondly, as will be shown presently, enhanced prestige or esteem is sometimes accorded on the basis of differential performance. Status rarely attaches to gross participation independently of the factors already discussed. Some interesting relationships between status and work, via the ideology of work, are reported occasionally in the literature, but with insufficient frequency for purposes of comparative analysis.

There is some indication, albeit highly speculative, that status may at times operate as a structural substitute for compensation, particularly in unbalanced familial-reciprocal organizations.

Some Typical Reward Situations

From the propositions set forth in this chapter, it is possible to construct a number of "ideal-typical" organizational and reward situations, if an ideal type is viewed as involving hypothetical extremes of established tendencies.

One such ideal type would be a custodial organization based on serfdom, tenancy, or peonage, with a balanced leiturgical reward system. Produce accumulates to the workers with part of the produce subsequently distributed to management on the basis of managerial proprietorship, combined with ascribed status differences and office differences. This situation is typical of the medieval European and Oriental feudal systems, and tenancy arrangements based on sharecropping.

Another such type would be a custodial *corvée*. The reward system might be unbalanced leiturgical, with accumulation of produce to management and no compensation. More likely, there would exist a balanced compensatory reward system in which part of the produce would be retained by management on the basis of managerial proprietorship and part distributed to the workers on the basis of gross participation, with compensation variable. This form is typical of both kinds of *corvées*. A variant of this form, characteristic of work on communal land, is for a smaller amount of accumulated produce to be retained by management on the basis of organization office (and possibly ascribed general status), with most of the produce distributed to the workers on the basis of corporate proprietorship.

A third ideal form is that typical of familial autonomous organizations, with unbalanced compensatory reward systems. Produce simply accumulates to the workers by virtue of gross participation but usually under conditions of managerial proprietorship.

There exist two kinds of typical familial-reciprocal situations. In the first kind—an unbalanced leiturgical system—produce accumulates to management on the basis of managerial proprietorship, and work is not compensated for. The second kind, which is the more common, involves a balanced compensatory reward system. Produce accumulates as before, but goods in kind are distributed to the workers on the basis of gross participation. Such compensation is either variable or fixed, and usually consists of food consumed on the spot.

In the ideal-typical familial-contractual organization, produce accumulates to management on the basis of managerial proprietorship, and money is distributed to the workers according to a fixed standard of performance.

Contractually based organizations ideally function in the same way. A variant occurs in the case of corporate proprietorship, where typically either all produce is distributed to workers on the added basis of corporate proprietorship, or else the produce is sold in its entirety by the organization and the proceeds in money are similarly distributed to the workers. The latter is of course similar to the modern industrial firm, except for the typical occurrence of corporate rather than separated proprietorship.

The last ideal type is that of the voluntary organization with a balanced compensatory reward system, in which produce accumulates to management and is then distributed to the workers in a variable way, on the basis of corporate proprietorship, differential performance, and sometimes organization office. This type, too, bears strong resemblances to that of the typical modern industrial firm.

These "constructed types" serve further to demonstrate problems of developing organizational forms appropriate to an industrial system in societies where large organizations tend to be custodial. For a shift from voluntary to custodial organizations implies a shift from compensatory to leiturgical reward systems, and a shift from a basis of differential performance to a basis of managerial proprietorship and ascribed status, in reward allocation. Furthermore, this shift away from an achievement emphasis in reward distribution is consistent with a declining relative functional importance of hunting as a source of food and an increasing relative functional importance of tillage, as has been shown earlier. For, from a technological viewpoint, competent performance is marginally less strategic in tillage than in the more complex forms of hunting. Thus a number of related factors appear to combine to form increasing organizational barriers to industrialization in "peasant," as opposed to "primitive," societies.

Incentives

Quite apart from rewards, there frequently appear to be elements inherent in the work situation itself which are institutionally expected to produce greater effort. Such elements will be termed *incentives.* Cross-cultural data on incentives have proved especially difficult to handle on a comparative basis. This is undoubtedly partly due to the fact that the motivation of human action as a general phenomenon is imperfectly understood, and thus there is no universally agreed upon way of reporting conditions institutionalized as "motivational." Since data on this score are extremely incomplete, much of the discussion following is based merely on general impressions. The classification of incentives is almost entirely *ad hoc,* and is made solely on the basis of distinctive behavior patterns in the work situation repeatedly characterized in descriptive monographs as making for, or expected to make for, greater effort. Five basic work patterns are from time to time reported, with allegations to the effect that they have motivational consequences, or at least are institutionally expected to have them: rhythm, competition, escape, expected differential allocation of rewards or status on the basis of work performance, and a fifth category which may appropriately be called "pleasure."

Rhythm

Rhythm, as a sociologically relevant phenomenon in work organization, is defined as a situation wherein several persons perform short-cycle repetitive activities in unison according to a common single time cycle. Rhythm is thus characteristic of combined effort, where it has consequences for coordination. However, there is some reason to believe that rhythm may be intrinsically motivating. According to Bücher and his later followers (Le Man, Maunier, and Friedmann, for example) rhythm produces a sort of frenetic inspiration making for a tendency for the pace to speed up.[9] Rhythm is occasionally reported explicitly as an incentive in tillage, where a line of workers may reap or hoe in unison. In the Dahomean *dokpwe,* and the Haitian *combite,* special drummers and songs are used.[10] Rhythm also similarly occurs in collection and in dwelling construction; no examples were found in other types of production.

Competition

Competition, defined in this context as a situation wherein any given person manifestly attempts to work harder than any other given person and is expected to do so, is reported from time to time as an incentive. It is frequently combined either with rhythm or with differential rewards or status based on work performance. Competition as reported in tillage usually involves two groups performing related work who attempt to "get ahead" of one another. In rice planting among the Betsileo, for example, the women attempt to plant shoots faster than the men can prepare the field ahead of them.[11] In fishing, competition is sometimes institutionalized in poisoning operations—each person present is expected to try to grab all the fish from the pool that he can and to keep others from doing the same thing where possible. Competition sometimes becomes intrinsic to the work situation through differential prestige or rewards attached to success, plus scarcity, as in the case of hunting among the Plains Indians.

Escape

Escape is defined as manifest departure from the routines of everyday life. As such, it is found institutionalized as an incentive in various production organizations. It appears most frequently in organizations involving expeditions away from the community, such as hunting parties, and is often surrounded with special rituals and supported by the use of special language during the period of escape. Scattered examples were found in hunting, fishing, collection, and tillage.

Differential Reward and Status Expectations

This incentive is closely connected with competition and is most often reported explicitly as an incentive in voluntary hunting organizations.

"Pleasure"

"Pleasure" is reported as an incentive whenever the ethnographer states in effect that his impression is that everyone working has a "good time," for reasons apparently independent of any of the above factors. Pleasure in work, in this sense, is variously alleged in tillage, hunting, fishing, and dwelling construction. Auxiliary workers, for example, often appear to enjoy themselves in familial-reciprocal organizations. And the tendency for certain organizations with unbalanced worker reward systems to assume recreational functions has already been noted.

NOTES TO CHAPTER SIX

1. This distinction is based on Weber's distinction between "leiturgi-cal," and "taxation," or "rational," methods of levying state funds. See Weber, *General Economic History*, 95, 336.

2. Following a similar line of reasoning, however, one would also expect American type *corvées* to tend to involve balanced compensatory reward systems relative to African types, which would involve unbalanced leiturgical systems. Although empirically in the expected direction, this relationship is not statistically significant:

	Balanced compensatory	Unbalanced leiturgical
American type *corvée*	10	2
African type *corvée*	7	6

$$Q = + .59 \qquad P = .123$$

3. In propositions 50, 51, 52, 58, and 63, separate samples were drawn in the same way described in Chapter One, but stratified so as to maximize the number of cases showing variation in the independent variables.

4. The idea of "balanced" exchange as a basis of stable social relationships was suggested by Professor George C. Homans of Harvard University, in a personal conversation. See Homans, *The Human Group*, 305-8, 421-3.

5. For example, Foster, *A Primitive Mexican Economy*, 34.

6. Herskovits, *Dahomey*, 63-77; *Life in a Haitian Valley*, 70-5.

7. Maunier, *Construction collective de la maison en Kabylie*, 65.

8. W. E. Moore, *Industrial Relations and the Social Order*, 258-62.

9. Bücher, *Arbeit und Rhytmus;* Friedmann, *Industrial Society*, 157-62.

10. Herskovits, *loci cit.*

11. DuBois, *Monographie des Betsileo*, 434-40.

ANCILLARY SYSTEMS

AN ANCILLARY SYSTEM is any pattern of action performed by members of a production organization which is not a part of the structure of division of labor, but which is culturally defined as essential to the technological process being carried on. Such systems of action are of some interest, inasmuch as they appear to be rather intimately connected with adjustment both to uncertainty and institutional contradictions. As has been shown in Chapter Two, adequate adjustment to uncertainty involves a capacity for decision-making in the absence of complete information, as well as some apparent ability to control or explain random influences on production. Adjustment to institutional contradictions involves the justification of technologically essential activity which tends otherwise to be culturally prohibited.

Decision-making

The assumption that production is essentially a rational activity is by no means inconsistent with the possibilities that certain decisions must be made for organizational reasons on grounds which are technologically arbitrary and that certain decisions must be made in the face of incomplete information. However, the presence of either or both of these conditions creates problems which, at least empirically, appear to be difficult of solution without recourse to procedures which are manifestly nonrational in character. The precise time at which production is to commence may, for example, be quite arbitrary from a technological standpoint, but at the same time be a matter which must be agreed upon in the interests of effective organization. Instances of manifestly random agreement on such matters are virtually never reported. Rather, such decisions are most frequently made by some ancillary system of action on the basis of nonrational criteria. What is interesting, however, is that the end result is the same. The ancillary systems concerned perform the latent function of making arbitrary decisions, but do so in a manner which does not have the appearance to the participants of being arbitrary.[1]

> In Western Tibet, plowing always begins sometime between the 8th and 22nd of May, which two dates are set by the position of the sun relative to certain prominent mountain peaks. The precise date within this range is set by astrology; the Lama names the auspicious day. In the case of literate farmers, he provides them with a chart to serve as a guide.
>
> Among the Trobriand Islanders, ". . . magic is a systematizing, regulating, and controlling influence in garden work. The magician, in carrying out the rites, sets the pace, compels people to apply themselves to certain tasks, and to accomplish them properly and in time. . . . There is no doubt that by its influence in ordering, systematizing, and regulating work, magic is economically invaluable to the natives." Some time in September, the garden magician announces the holding of a garden council. The council, composed of the men of the village, meets the next day. The chief and garden magician explain how garden land is to be allocated, and signal the beginning of planting.
>
> Among the Iroquois, agricultural routine was marked by a series of seasonal festivals, in terms of which activities could be coordinated.
>
> Among the Thai, plowing is initiated at the beginning of the rainy season by ceremonial plowing by an official, combined with measures to keep evil spirits away from the fields. A similar "First Furrow" ceremony is reported throughout the Far East.[2]

A similar pattern is often encountered in making decisions between alternative courses of action in the absence of information sufficiently adequate to enable a sure choice. Instances of manifest randomization of strategy under such circumstances are lacking. However, various ancillary systems involving nonrational procedures are very common indeed, and are interesting because they seem to lead to precisely the same result while at the same time not appearing to be random to the participants themselves. Perhaps the most important such practice is divination. The Lobi Chief of the Hunt, for example, determines the time and direction of search parties in hunting by consulting the entrails of a chicken. The latent result is randomization of strategy.[3]

The explanation as to why such decision-making mechanisms should so often assume a form which is manifestly religious or magical is by no means sure, but certain studied speculations can be made on this score. No social system can withstand extreme unpredictability. The use of magic and religion as aids in making essentially arbitrary decisions has the advantage of lending a deterministic character to the proceedings. It also provides a ready means for the explanation of failure, particularly where the magic is culturally defined as "volitional," as will be explained in the succeeding section. It furthermore is self-justifying even from a pragmatic standpoint, since to the degree that the end result is in fact randomization of strategy, it "works" in a very real sense.

Control

Attempts to control the external environment by means of magic in the face of uncertainty are so widespread and have been so widely commented on that they hardly require special mention.

> Among the Hopi, rain-making and inducement of soil fertility involve setting up shrines in the field upon completion of clearing. Special ceremonies are performed by the *Katcina* society to insure fertility. Sprouts are likewise ceremonially planted by the society in order to prolong the summer. The clansfolk of the Sunwatcher give prayer-sticks to a boy at the summer solstice; he arranges them in the field, and walks home very slowly in order that the sun may advance more slowly and the summer be prolonged. On the first day of planting, a man is doused with water in order to produce abundant water in the fields.[4]

That the existence of such routinized procedures designed to control the external environment is universal is undoubted. The fact that supernatural appeals are made in connection with many such procedures is similarly undoubted. However, there appears to be a certain confusion in the literature between religion, magic, and science in discussions of procedures such as the above. In the recent literature it has been commonly held, at least implicitly, that all magical activities involve some orientation to and belief in supernatural powers. The wholesale interpretation of magic as "bad science," in Frazer's term, has indeed been shown to be untenable; however, the wholesale interpretation of magic as "religious engineering" appears similarly to be possibly incorrect.[5] In many societies there appear to be two categories of magic, as viewed by the participants themselves. The first type may be termed "volitional." It is characterized by an appeal to supernatural forces to intervene in the manipulation of the physical world. Such forces are conceived to be endowed with the quality of volition; they may choose to intervene or they may not. Failure is relatively easy to explain on the grounds that such powers chose not to intervene. The Christian belief that God answers petitions at His own pleasure as He sees fit would be an example of belief in "volitional magic."

The other type of magic may be termed "sympathetic," after Frazer's usage. It is essentially "bad science" and is reducible to ignorance or error. It involves simply a conceived association between events: if event A is performed, event B will result. If any intervening forces are conceived at all, they are not viewed as endowed with the power of volition. Failure is characteristically explained on the grounds that event A was not performed properly.

It is certainly not the case that all magical observances can be made to fit neatly into one or the other of these two categories. As will be shown presently, elements of both types may be involved—although not necessarily. What is being argued is that two qualitatively different subjective orientations may be involved. The first is religious; the second, scientific. "Magic" does not exist independently as a system of thought; it is, rather, a form of engineering of either a religious or a "bad" scientific sort, as the case may be.[6] This distinction, moreover, appears to have some predictive implications for organizational structure.

The idea of a universal distinction between volitional magic, on the one hand, and science in general, on the other, is today generally accepted. As Malinowski puts it, with reference to the Trobriand Islanders:

"The two ways, the way of magic and the way of garden work—*megwa la keda, bagula la keda*—are inseparable. They are never confused, nor is one of them ever allowed to supersede the other. The natives will never try to clean the soil by magic, to erect a fence or yam support by a rite. They know quite well that they have to do it by hand and in the sweat of their brow. They also know that no work can be skimped without danger to the crops, nor do they ever assume that by an overdose of magic you can make good any deficiencies in work."[7]

The view that distinctions are made between volitional and sympathetic magic is less easily supported. Seligman expresses this view, stating that among the Veddas an explicit distinction is made between ". . . ceremonies and observances . . . which depend for their efficacy upon the successful appeal to some extra-human personal influence," and ". . . actions which are expected to produce the required result automatically by virtue of their own intrinsic qualities."[8] There is some evidence of almost purely sympathetic magic apparently devoid of religious significance in various cultures. Charms used in hunting and fishing often seem to fall in this category; they simply "attract" game or fish.

> Among the Jivaro, certain stones are used to attract fish. The Jivaro explain their use by saying that the stones are often found in the stomachs of the fish, who are therefore attracted by the stones. The Cuna employ similar charms to catch turtles; songs are likewise sung for the same purpose.[9]

Animal charming is, on the other hand, likely to involve volitional elements as well.

> The Aleut believe in the transmigration of human male souls into seals. They therefore try to attract seals by adorning boats with human female clothing, stating the above belief as the reason for this.[10]

It is possible that further research would reveal a genuine difference of the sort described on a fairly large cross-cultural scale—a difference which would not be without organizational implications. Religious reinforcement involving volitional magic is frequently associated with custodial organization, in that officials may be believed to have special connections with supernatural powers. The hypothesis is suggested that, under custodial forms, sympathetic magic tends to shift to volitional magic. As a consequence, production becomes less scientifically oriented; the position of those in authority becomes more secure; and their mistakes are more easily explained.

Justification

As explained earlier, inadequate institutionalization may in extreme cases extend to a condition wherein technologically essential activities are institutionally prohibited. For example, the killing of fish is supposedly prohibited by the Buddhist religion, yet fishing is fairly widespread in many Buddhist societies. Situations of this type imply the existence of some mechanism which resolves the apparent contradictions in such a way that the necessary procedures are at least to some extent culturally justified. Such mechanisms often assume the form of ancillary systems of action.

> Among the Thai, spirits must be driven out of wild elephants before they can be hunted, to free the animal from his obligations to the wild herd; this is done by an elaborate ceremony.
> Among the Jukun, when a fishing party ventures forth, "the first duty is the propitiation of the spirits which haunt the surroundings." Similarly, the Malay must placate the sea spirits (*hantu laut*) before fishing can begin.[11]
> Also, "in all of Indochina rituals mark the danger of any move that would be sacrilege against the earth . . . there are also, says Aymonier, 'ideas that it is a crime to tear up and seed the earth'; therefore, as of the first cock-crow friends go out on the propitious day and secretly dig three furrows in complete silence around the plot devoted by each peasant to the gods. At dawn the owner of the lands wanders over in that direction as though by the merest chance. At the sight of the furrows he stops, feints vivid surprise and says, 'who could have come and secretly worked my fields during the night?' He hastens to make offerings to the gods, asking them to forgive the unknown who came to work his fields and to give him good harvests; from then on he can plough his fields without fear."[12]

In Buddhist societies, such negation often takes the form of a rationalization. The Buddhist faith theoretically forbids the killing of any living thing. Fishermen, consequently, either take great pains to keep their catch alive until it is sold, or else make certain the fish is alive when it is removed from the hook. The latter precaution enables them to claim that they are not responsible; the fish, when left on land, simply died of its own accord.[13]

Ancillary Systems and Organization Structure

Unevenness in the data does not permit any definitive generalizations concerning the implications of ancilliary systems for organizational structure. In general, there are some indications that ancillary functions are likely to be performed by organization members under custodial conditions, and likely to be performed by outside specialists in other types of organization.

Ancillary systems frequently operate to make random decisions. It also appears that religious beliefs engender practices which take time from technological activities either in the form of attempts to control the environment or to negate contradictory institutionalization. The organizational consequences of this could not be determined with any precision. It appears that in custodial organizations, such functions may be performed by officials who are high in the hierarchy; that custodial organizations are likely to involve volitional rather than sympathetic elements in such a way as to reinforce the position of the official. In other types of organizations, outside specialists appear to be used, except in the performance of the most exoteric rites. In either case, organizational structure does not seem to be affected so much as does the length of time required for the process to be performed.

NOTE TO CHAPTER SEVEN

1. See Kochen and Levy, "The Logical Nature of an Action Scheme," *Behavioral Science,* I, 281. Also, O. K. Moore, "Divination—a New Perspective," *American Anthropologist,* LIX, 69-74.

2. *Gazeteer of the Kangra District,* II, 108-9; Asboe, "Farmers and Farming in Ladakh. . .," *Journal of the Royal Central Asian Society,* XXXIV, 188; Malinowski, *Argonauts of the Western Pacific,* 60; *Coral Gardens and their Magic,* 87-93; Morgan, *League of the Ho-de-no-sau-nee,* I, 175-217; Landon, *Thailand in Transition,* 236-9; Graham, *Siam,* II, 265-78; Brodrick, *Little Vehicle,* 238-9; Poree and Maspero, *Moeurs et coutumes der Kmers,* 154-5.

3. Labouret, *Les tribus du rameau Lobi,* 123. For this basic posture the author is largely indebted to O. K. Moore, *loc. cit.*

4. Forde, "Hopi Agriculture and Land Ownership," *Journal of the Royal Anthropological Institute,* XLI, 388-9.

5. Frazer, *The Golden Bough* (abridged edition), 11-45; Malinowski, *Magic, Science, and Religion;* also see Goode, *Religion among the Primitives.*

6. There are likewise various gradations and overlaps between "scientific magic" and accepted standard engineering practice. An example of an intermediate type would be "rules of thumb." Furthermore, as some of the examples below will illustrate, it is by no means certain that all "bad science" is really so "bad."

7. Malinowski, *Coral Gardens and their Magic,* 76.

8. Seligman, *The Veddas,* 190.

9. Karsten, *The Head-Hunters of Western Amazonas,* 180; Dens-

more, *Music of the Tule Indians of Panama*, 26-8. It is not altogether clear that these practices—particularly the Jivaro example—constitute "bad" science, as anyone who has ever done any fishing can well imagine.

10. Ivanov, "Aleut Hunting Headgear and its Ornamentation," *Proceedings of the 23rd International Congress of Americanists*, 482-500.

11. Srichandrakumara, "Adversaria of Elephant Hunting. . .," *Journal of the Siam Society*, XXIII, 74; Meek, *A Sudanese Kingdom*, 425; Firth, *Malay Fishermen*, 122-5.

12. Brodrick, *op. cit.*, 155.

13. Scott, *The Burman*, 285, 343.

8

CONCLUSIONS

As EXPLAINED IN CHAPTER ONE, this investigation has been conducted within the framework of two working hypotheses:

A. *The structure of any production organization is determined partly by the characteristics of the technological process which it is carrying on, and partly by the social setting within which it exists.*

B. *The structure of any reward system is determined partly by the characteristics of the production organization involved, and partly by the social setting, within limits imposed by features of the technological process.*

As stated earlier, the purpose of this study has not been to discover whether these hypotheses are valid as such; few if any social scientists would take issue with them in the form stated. Rather, the purpose has been to discover the precise conditions under which, and the precise respects in which, each of the alternatives stated in these hypotheses will hold as opposed to another of the alternatives. The investigation has thus developed 64 propositions which attempt to clarify the determinants of production organization and reward system structure. These 64 propositions represent generalizations of a lower order than that of the original two working hypotheses; essentially, they are statements of statistical covariation of substructures of technological process, production organization, social setting, and reward system. The results may be summarized, then, by specifying the conditions of each working hypothesis and stating the respects in which each alternative has been found to apply. This will be done, first of all, by a general statement, and secondly, by stating each relevant proposition developed.

Verified Conclusions: Hypothesis A

The structure of any production organization is determined partly by the characteristics of the technological process which it is carrying on, and partly by the social setting within which it exists.

Given a systematization of the possible range of variation of technological processes, it was found that certain aspects of authority, division of labor, solidarity, proprietorship, and recruitment structure could be predicted as to general trend from technology alone. In addition, extremely strong internal structural-functional consistencies were found between dimensions of these five areas, thus making for more marked relationships than might otherwise have been the case. However, certain systematic exceptions to the over-all relationships between technology and organization readily became apparent, and again even more marked than one might expect, owing to internal structural consistencies. Such exceptions are presumably to be explained culturally. On this score, it was found that much of the technologically unexplained variation could be accounted for by the political structure of the society concerned; predominantly political influences, under certain conditions, tend to override technological considerations in determining organizational structure.

Range of Technological Variation

Nonindustrial technological processes may be oriented to tillage, hunting, fishing, collection, construction, animal husbandry, or manufacturing. Variations between these types may be described in terms of the dimensions of complexity, work load, outlay, and uncertainty. In this regard:

1. *Tillage and construction are more complex in task structure than are hunting, fishing, and collection.*

2. *Hunting is more complex with respect to combined effort than is fishing, collection, or construction.*

3. *Tillage is more complex with respect to combined effort than is collection.*

4. *In total degree of complexity, tillage and construction are more complex than hunting, and hunting is more complex than fishing or collection.*

5. *Tillage and construction tend to be characterized by variable work loads; hunting, fishing, and collection, by constant work loads.*

In addition, tillage and construction appear to involve tending and manipulation of raw materials, respectively, with such randomness as occurs taking place in areas where the process is not understood; whereas hunting and fishing involve manipulation of raw materials with the necessity of controlling randomness by increased attention paid to the process. Tillage and construction require small, fixed land areas, while hunting, fishing, and collection tend to involve larger land areas with diffuse access generally necessary.

Technological Determinants of Organizational Structure

The above technological differences account to a considerable extent for differences in organization structure. The major intervening variables appear to be fluctuation in the amount and total duration of effort required during a process, as reflected by length of process and variation in work load, the amount of attention required by a process as determined by its complexity, and the uncertainty of raw material behavior.

Length of process and work load variation is reflected organizationally as follows:

14. Tillage, construction, animal husbandry, and manufacturing tend to be carried on by permanent organizations; hunting, fishing, and collection, by temporary organizations.

15. Tillage and construction tend to be carried on by basic-auxiliary organizations; hunting, fishing, and collection, by autonomous organizations.

Complexity is reflected principally in authority structure:

6. Construction organizations are relatively more likely to be bureaucratic than are organizations carrying on other processes.

7. Organizations carrying on complex processes tend to be bureaucratic; whereas organizations carrying on simple processes tend to be associational.

The degree of attention occasioned by uncertainty of raw material behavior is reflected largely in the structure of division of labor, and, in turn, in recruitment criteria:

11. Hunting and fishing tend to be carried on by organizations emphasizing specificity; tillage, animal husbandry, and construction, by organizations emphasizing diffuseness.

12. Hunting and fishing tend to be carried on by organizations emphasizing achievement; tillage, animal husbandry, and construction, by organizations emphasizing ascription.

128

17. *Hunting organizations tend to be based on territorial recruitment; tillage and construction organizations, on social recruitment.*

Type of land area required is reflected in that:

16. *Tillage and construction are associated with managerial or separated proprietorship; hunting, fishing, and collection, with corporate proprietorship.*

Consistency in Organizational Structure

Organizational structure may be bureaucratic or associational as to authority, specific or diffuse and achievement or ascription centered as to division of labor, and permanent or temporary and autonomous or basic-auxiliary as to solidarity. In addition, production organizations may be based on managerial, separated, or corporate proprietorship and may involve territorial or social recruitment. Over-all relationships between technology and these dimensions of organizational structure have just been noted. In addition, these structural dimensions exhibit certain striking relationships among themselves:

20. *Temporary organizations tend to be specific, territorially recruited, and autonomous.*

21. *Specific organizations tend to be territorially recruited and autonomous.*

22. *Territorially recruited organizations tend to be autonomous.*

23. *Basic-auxiliary organizations tend to be permanent, diffuse, and socially recruited.*

24. *Basic-auxiliary organizations tend to involve managerial or separated proprietorship.*

25. *Achievement tends to be emphasized in specific, territorially recruited autonomous organizations.*[1]

26. *Among autonomous organizations, corporate proprietorship is associated with territorial recruitment.*

It is significant that the association-bureaucracy dimension is not related to any of the other principal organizational dimensions. Thus, the existence of bureaucracy alone in nonindustrial culture does not guarantee "rational" administration. However, bureaucracy does tend to involve certain other attributes often alleged to be associated with it:

8. *In bureaucracies, managers are likely not to work, while in associations managers are likely to work.*

9. *Bureaucracies are more likely than associations to distribute rewards to members in return for participation.*

10. *In organizations where rewards are distributed to members, the quantity of the reward tends to vary according to organization office in bureaucracies, but not in associations.*

Social Determinants of Organizational Structure

The pattern of exceptions to over-all relationships between technology and organization reveals that a great many hunting and fishing organizations are in fact permanent, rather than temporary; diffuse, rather than specific; ascription rather than achievement centered; socially rather than territorially recruited; and managerial or separated, rather than corporate, as to proprietorship. Furthermore, the internal consistencies revealed in organizational structure indicate that such exceptions are systematically combined in the same organizations, rather than scattered at random. In addition, a rather unaccountably large number of tillage and construction organizations are autonomous rather than basic-auxiliary. Such exceptions presumably are explicable on social grounds, and thus provide a key to the social determinants of organization structure. The principal link between society and organization is to be found in the structure of recruitment. Four major institutional types of production organization could be discerned, on the basis of recruitment patterns: familial, custodial, contractual, and voluntary. These four institutional types are related to the organizational dimensions set forth above as follows:

27. *Familial organizations tend to be basic-auxiliary, diffuse, and permanent.*

28. *Custodial organizations tend to be autonomous, diffuse, and permanent.*

29. *Contractual organizations tend to be autonomous, specific, and permanent.*

30. *Voluntary organizations tend to be autonomous, specific, and temporary.*

31. *Custodial organizations tend to be bureaucratic.*

32. *Contractual and voluntary organizations tend to emphasize achievement.*

33. *Familial and custodial organizations tend to involve managerial or separated proprietorship; contractual and voluntary organizations, corporate proprietorship.*

Relationships between institutional types and technology are as one would expect, in view of the above:

34. *Tillage, construction, and animal husbandry tend to be carried on by custodial or familial organizations.*

35. *Hunting, fishing, and collection tend to be carried on by voluntary organizations.*

36. *If hunting and fishing are not carried on by voluntary organizations, they tend to be carried on by custodial organizations.*

Thus the original problem posed by exceptional cases reduces to the question of why so much hunting and fishing is custodially organized, in view of the fact that such organization is literally the opposite of what one would expect on purely technological grounds. In addition, one may inquire as to the conditions under which tillage and construction are custodially, rather than familially, organized. Similarly, the question arises as to why contractual organization does not occur more frequently than it does, since it is better suited technologically to hunting and fishing than is the custodial form.

The key social variable involved in these problems appears to be the presence or absence of a centralized government in the society concerned:

37. *Custodial and contractual organizations tend to exist only in societies having centralized governments.*

38. *Under conditions of centralized government, hunting and fishing tend to be carried on by custodial, rather than voluntary, organizations.*

39. *Under conditions of centralized government, tillage, construction, and animal husbandry tend to be carried on by custodial, rather than familial, organizations*

The circumstances of propositions 38 and 39, however, are different. For:

40. *Voluntary organization is negatively associated with centralized government.*

41. *If custodial organizations are present, voluntary organizations tend to be absent, in the same society.*

Thus, under conditions of centralized government, custodial organization tends to occur in all types of production, irrespective of technological suitability. At the same time, voluntary organizations tend to disappear, while familial forms remain, coexistent with custodial types. The reason why contractual forms do not tend to appear with such vigor seems to lie in the mechanism involved in the establishment and diffusion of custodial forms. Briefly, it appears that custodial organization requires some ultimate central authority for its base. Such authority may be vested in the government itself, or in a general stratification system ultimately associated with the government. For:

45. Societies with centralized governments are more likely to possess complex hierarchies of general social stratification than are societies without centralized government.

Once established, it would seem that custodial forms tend to become diffused to all types of production by virtue of the fact that control over outlay in resources is vested in the same structure as is centralized political authority:

43. In societies with centralized government, production organizations are characterized by managerial or separated, rather than corporate, proprietorship.

The fact that an agricultural surplus is generally present under such conditions may be presumed to offset the probable loss of efficiency in hunting and fishing occasioned by the use of custodial organizations:

42. Societies with centralized governments tend to practice settled agriculture.

Contractual organization does not exhibit a like tendency; there is no reason to suppose from its institutional basis that it would:

44. Custodial organization is more likely to occur in more than one type of process in the same society than is contractual organization.

Hypothesis A, therefore, may be said to hold true in the respects indicated.

Verified Conclusions: Hypothesis B

The structure of any reward system is determined partly by the characteristics of the production organization involved, and partly by the social setting, within limits imposed by features of the technological process.

Any reward system involves the allocation of produce, and may also involve the allocation of money and/or goods in kind. Four basic types of reward systems may be distinguished, according to pattern of allocation: balanced compensatory, balanced leiturgical, unbalanced compensatory, and unbalanced leiturgical. Rewards may be allocated by criteria based on proprietorship, gross participation, achievement, organization office, or status ascribed independently of the production organization.

Technological limits of reward systems stem from the physical nature of certain types of processes, which permit produce to accumulate only in certain ways. Thus:

46. Tillage, hunting, construction, and manufacturing tend to be characterized by balanced compensatory or unbalanced leiturgical reward systems; while fishing, collection, and animal husbandry tend to be characterized, relatively, by unbalanced compensatory or balanced leiturgical reward systems.

47. In balanced reward systems, goods in kind are more likely to be distributed in tillage and construction; produce, in hunting, fishing, and collection.

It may be hypothesized that within these limits, the nature of any reward system is determined both by organizational as well as social influences in that rewards tend to be structured in such a way as to "compensate for" institutional inadequacies in the areas of motivation and cognition. Considerable support is given this hypothesis by the fact that many variations in reward systems are associated with variations in the nature of such inadequacies, in a way which would be implied by the hypothesis. Thus:

48. Bureaucracies tend to possess balanced reward systems; associations, unbalanced reward systems.

49. Voluntary organizations and organizations with basic or auxiliary contractual elements tend to possess balanced compensatory reward systems.

50. Familial-reciprocal organizations and custodial corvées tend to be characterized by unbalanced leiturgical reward systems.

51. Bolhon type organizations tend to involve unbalanced leiturgical systems relative to palihog types, which are relatively more likely to involve balanced compensatory systems.

52. Serfdom, tenancy, and peonage tend toward balanced leiturgical reward systems.

53. Familial autonomous organizations tend to be characterized by unbalanced compensatory reward systems.

62. Among organizations where rewards are distributed, familial-reciprocal forms tend to be characterized by distribution on the basis of gross participation only.

63. Rewards based on achievement tend to consist of money; rewards based on other criteria tend to consist of produce and goods in kind.

64. In custodial and voluntary bureaucracies with rewards differentiated by office, the greater the amount of authority attached to the office, the greater the amount of the reward.

The theory advanced earlier alleging the crucial nature of control over resources in the determination of organizational structure is further supported by the following propositions regarding rewards:

59. Except in the case of familial autonomous organizations, some ultimate allocation of some item always occurs on the basis of proprietorship.

60. Except for familial autonomous types, organizations with managerial proprietorship always involve accumulation or distribution to management.

61. Organizations with corporate proprietorship always involve accumulation or distribution to the workers.

Propositions concerning reward items follow from certain propositions preceding:

54. In an unbalanced leiturgical reward system, rewards consist solely of produce, which accumulates to management.

55. In an unbalanced compensatory reward system, rewards consist solely of produce, which accumulates to the workers.

56. In custodial or voluntary organizations with balanced systems, produce tends to be used as a distribution item, rather than money or goods in kind.

57. In familial organizations with balanced systems, money or goods in kind tend to be used as distribution items, rather than produce.

58. In balanced systems involving either basic or auxiliary contractual elements in the organization, money tends to be used as a distribution item.

Thus hypothesis B may be regarded as valid in the respects and under the conditions indicated. In the remainder of this chapter, possible broader implications of the findings will be explored.

Cultural Uniformity and Diversity

It is possible to interpret the history of comparative social analysis as a sort of dialectic between two "schools." The first "school" of thought stresses cultural uniformities; the second, cultural diversity. The evolutionist "comparative approach," for example, assumed essentially that all human cultures are the same. Observed differences were to be explained by assigning the cultures in question to different "stages" of development, the implication being that different cultures at the same "stage" will exhibit like characteristics. That such a position is untenable has certainly been adequately demonstrated over the past forty years. Whatever the empirical merits of the older "comparative approach," however, the fact remains that it did involve two notable characteristics of "posture." In the first place, it tended to draw attention to uniformities common to all cultures. Secondly, it involved the assumption that certain aspects of any given culture could be adequately explained without knowing "everything" about the culture concerned. In contrast, the later doctrine of "cultural relativism," undoubtedly in part as a quite understandable reaction to evolutionistic thought, lay an extremely heavy emphasis on cultural diversity. It drew attention away from cultural uniformities, and stressed cultural differences. Carried to extremes, the doctrine of "cultural relativism" asserts that each culture is unique, and that no one trait of any given culture can be explained without at the same time knowing and explaining "everything" about the culture concerned.

The results of the present study are not in accord with this view. Cultural uniformities do exist and furthermore can be understood on a comparative basis without treating the cultures concerned as "wholes." Propositions 1-36 and 46-47 state relationships which are not culturally relative. Some of these relationships hold by virtue of physical-technological limitations combined with constants of human biology, but others—notably those concerned with internal structural consistencies of organizations—appear to be predominantly social in nature. The remaining propositions are all concerned in one way or another with cultural diversity, yet it is clear in these respects that no culture is "completely" different from every other culture. Furthermore, at no point is it necessary for purposes of this study to deal with any culture as a "whole."

The present study suggests, therefore, that technological limitations on the possible forms which successful instrumental action can take, together with limitations as to interrelationships between such forms, constitute major sources of cross-cultural uniformity. Not just any kind of culturally approved organizational form is possible. Furthermore, to the extent that these results are adjudged to have any merit at all, this study indicates that comparative study of selected aspects of culture, without reference to other aspects irrelevant to the purpose at hand, is entirely feasible.

Administrative Theory

One of the most difficult problems of complex organization theory is the development of models which are not "self-contained"; i.e., which do not assume an organization operating in a vacuum or in a setting which is held constant. To be sure, the lack of such models is not equally important to all areas of administrative research. That relationships between the organization and its social setting are unquestionably relevant to a vast range of problems, however, has certainly been adequately demonstrated by much "human relations" research. The lack of appropriate models to deal with this range of problems is demonstrated by the frequent use in this area, *faute de mieux*, of models which are really inappropriate to the problems being investigated. Thus, through no particular fault of the investigators, the use of self-contained models in studies which deal essentially with relationships between the organization and its setting is often attempted for want of a better approach, with the result that most of the variables in which one is interested are not contained in the conceptual scheme employed, but must be lumped together in an additional category called "informal organization." Clearly, the situation of having to adduce a residual category to explain the phenomena in which one is interested is far from ideal, and suggests the use of a different model altogether.

Models of formal organization which explicitly and systematically include aspects of the social setting are obviously not to be developed overnight. The present study, however, perhaps suggests some possible approaches to this problem. The most general parameters here used are technology, organization structure, social setting, and reward system. Relevant aspects of technology are complexity, work load, outlay, and uncertainty; of organization structure, authority (number of levels), division of labor (comprising the dimensions of specificity-diffuseness and achievement-ascription, as well as amount), solidarity (permanent-temporary and autonomous-basic-auxiliary organization), proprietorship (managerial-separated-corporate), and recruitment (territorial-social). The property system and the political system appear as the most significant features of the social setting, and four basic kinds of reward patterns are delineated. The major problem focused on is the way in which the social setting is related to organization structure, within limits imposed by technology. In the model suggested by the findings, technological complexity sets limits on the number of levels of authority and the amount of division of labor; work load sets limits on both dimensions of solidarity: outlay combined with uncertainty poses limitations on both dimensions of kind of division of labor; and territorial outlay limits the mode of proprietorship indirectly through differential difficulty of institutionalizing control over property. In addition, certain intrinsic consistencies appear between the structures of division of labor, solidarity, and recruitment which increase the technological implications for organization and render problems of institutionalization more clear-cut. The central point of the model thus emerges as the problem of institutionalizing relationships which tend to be required by virtue of technology combined with exigencies of organizational consistency. By the model, such institutionalization is accomplished primarily through the ways in which the property and political systems act on the structure of recruitment. Unlike most other models of administrative structure, it is assumed here that such institutionalization has a tendency to be inadequate both from a cognitive as well as a motivational standpoint. Institutional "deficiencies" have two basic consequences, again in terms of the model. In the first place, they may result in a decline of over-all efficiency, brought about through an alteration of the recruitment, and hence the solidarity and division of labor, patterns. Secondly, they may be at least partially "compensated for" by the use of a balanced reward system which aids in the institutionalization of both adequate cognition and motivation. The affinity of the result to criteria for "rational" administration is a matter to be determined empirically, and, by the model, is subject to a wide range of variation.

No claim is made here that any definitive model has been developed. Rather, attention is called to the fact that the findings are perfectly consistent with the relationships alleged in the above broad outline, which avoids reliance on the rather vague, residual category of "informal organization." Further research along these lines could perhaps result in the development of an administrative model better suited than existing models to many current problems of organizational research.

Implications for Industrial Development

On a more concrete level, the findings presented here, if they are valid, have some rather disturbing implications for prospects of economic development of underdeveloped areas. Industrialism, so far as is known, depends on contractual production organization. The present findings indicate that, while conditions making for production organization based on specificity, achievement, territorial recruitment, and balanced compensatory reward systems are by no means absent in nonindustrial societies, they are not particularly likely to be present in today's typical nonindustrial society about to attempt industrialization. Such societies are by and large of the "peasant" variety; that is, they possess organized agriculture combined with a centralized government. Specificity, achievement, and balanced worker rewards, however, are more likely to be found in production organizations characteristic of "primitive," or "tribal," societies. The probable relationship between the political system and land tenure arrangements in "peasant" societies appears to result in the disappearance of organizations of this sort in favor of custodial forms, involving diffuseness, ascription, and leiturgical reward systems. The development of permanent contractual organizations on a large scale under such conditions seems to be difficult. Such contractual organizations as were observed appear largely to be associations of small proprietors or peasants set up for the purpose of providing ancillary services to other production organizations which are not contractually organized. It is true that the circulation of money is associated with the existence of contractual elements. But such elements often serve as auxiliaries to familial organizations rather than as basic core elements of contractual organizations per se. One seems to be faced with the fact that the prerequisites to industrialism centering around political order at the same time set forces in motion which result in existing organizational forms becoming further removed from those essential to an industrial system, rather than more adapted to industrialism. With the advent of a general medium of exchange, the problem appears to be one of reversing this trend. The existence of money apparently makes contractual organization easier, but the problem of an over-all shift from control through land to control through finance still remains difficult.

Industrial development, therefore, involves not so much the problem of developing large bureaucratic organizational forms as it involves the problem of devising appropriate modes of institutionalizing such forms. The extent to which it is possible for a custodial organization to be changed by design into a contractual structure is difficult to assess. Some historical examples of such attempts were uncovered during the course of research. In the

138

latter years of the Roman Empire, slave revolts and increasing shortages of servile labor led to some efforts to reform the *latifundia* in this way. Such attempts were unsuccessful largely owing to the difficulty of turning tenants into subcontractors in a context of fiefs and benefices. The result was that the *coloni* tended to become peons rather than free contract laborers, and the ultimate consequence was merely another kind of custodial organization.[2] A similar chain of events has been noted in connection with land reform attempts in early twentieth-century Persia.[3] It may well be true that custodial organizations cannot be changed directly into contractual types. Such a change at least raises the question of whether existing role assignment under a custodial system is sufficiently in accord with ability to do the work in a contractual system. If such a shift is impossible, industrialization of certain areas may prove to require extreme disruption of existing landed property arrangements, in order to permit concentration on development of indigenous corporate contractual forms, and allow for the development of a generalized system of financial control.

NOTES TO CHAPTER EIGHT

1. See also propositions *13* and *18* in this connection.
2. Cary, *A History of Rome*, 257-60, 451-2, 561-2, 666 ff.
3. Lambton, *Landlord and Peasant in Persia*. Further research into historical instances of attempts to change the form of custodial organization would undoubtedly prove illuminating on this score.

Summary of Empirical Data

The Summary Table below lists the 150 societies investigated in detail, summarizing the salient data abstracted on each production system studied, with appropriate bibliographical references. As is indicated, the data are arrayed in eleven columns, numbered "A" through "K," and described by one or more digits in each column.

Key to Summary Table

COLUMN A: LOCATION OF SOCIETY*

1st digit	1 Africa	2 Circum-Mediterranean	3 East Eurasia
2nd digit			
1	Pygmies and Khoisan	Horn and Ethiopia	Middle East
2	Southern Bantu	Moslem Sudan	Central Asia
3	Central Bantu	Sahara	Arctic Asia
4	Northeast Bantu	North Africa	East Asia
5	Equatorial Bantu	Southern Europe	Himalayas
6	Guinea Coast	Overseas Europeans	North and Central India
7	Western Sudan	Northwest Europe	South India
8	Nigerian Plateau	Eastern Europe	Indian Ocean
9	Eastern Sudan	Caucasia	Assam and Burma
0	Upper Nile	Near East	Southeast Asia

	4 Insular Pacific	5 North America	6 South America
1	Philippines and Formosa	Arctic America	Central America
2	Western Indonesia	Northwest Coast	Caribbean
3	Eastern Indonesia	California	Guiana
4	Australia	Great Basin— Plateau	Lower Amazon
5	New Guinea	Plains	Interior Amazon
6	Micronesia	Prairie	Andes
7	Western Melanesia	Eastern Woodlands	Chile and Patagonia
8	Eastern Melanesia	Southwest	Gran Chaco
9	Western Polynesia	Northwest Mexico	Mato Grosso
0	Eastern Polynesia	Central Mexico	Eastern Brazil

*The scheme employed is that of G. P. Murdock, "World Ethnographic Sample," *American Anthropologist*, LIX (1957), 664-687.

COLUMN B:
SELECTED CULTURAL CHARACTERISTICS OF SOCIETY

1st digit	2nd digit	3rd digit
Agriculture	Stratification	Political Structure
1 absent or insignificant	1 formal age-grades	1 autonomous local
2 unimportant	2 complex	2 dependent
3 present and important	3 hereditary	3 little state
0 no data	aristocracy	4 minimal state
	4 none significant	5 none
	5 wealth only	6 peace group
	0 no data	7 state
		0 no data

Information in columns A and B is given only once for each society,
under the first entry, and is not repeated in successive entries.

COLUMN C: TECHNOLOGY

1st digit	2nd digit	3rd digit
Type of process	Work load	Complexity
1 tillage	1 variable	1 simple
2 hunting	2 constant	2 complex
3 fishing	0 no data	0 no data
4 collection		
5 animal husbandry		
6 construction		
7 manufacturing		
8 other		
0 no data		

COLUMN D: AUTHORITY

1st digit	2nd digit
Structural type	Managerial activity
1 association	1 all managers work
2 bureaucracy	2 at least some managers do not work
0 no data	0 no data

COLUMN E: DIVISION OF LABOR

1st digit	2nd digit
Substantive definition	Performance evaluation
1 specificity	1 achievement present in some respect
2 diffuseness	2 achievement not present
0 no data	0 no data

COLUMN F: SOLIDARITY

1st digit — Strength
1 permanent
2 temporary
0 no data

2nd digit — Variability
1 autonomous
2 basic-auxiliary
0 no data

COLUMN G: PROPRIETORSHIP

1 managerial
2 corporate
3 separated
0 no data

COLUMN H: RECRUITMENT AND INSTITUTIONAL TYPE

1st digit — General type
1 custodial autonomous
2 custodial-contractual
3 familial autonomous
4 familial-contractual
5 familial-reciprocal
6 familial-familial
7 contractual autonomous
8 contractual-other
9 voluntary autonomous
0 other or no data

2nd digit — Basic subtype
1 African *corvée*, small family, agency, or leader recruited, as applicable
2 American *corvée*, large family, managerial prop. type, leader elected, as applicable
3. serfdom or casual, as applicable
4 tenancy
5 peonage
6 slavery
7 total mobilization
0 no data

3rd digit — Auxiliary subtype
1 agency or *bolhon*, as applicable
2 individual or *palihog*, as applic.
3 familial
4 some variety of contractual, exact form undetermined
5 no auxiliary present
6 unique
0 present, no further data

COLUMN I: TYPE OF REWARD SYSTEM

1 balanced compensatory
2 unbalanced compensatory
3 balanced leiturgical
4 unbalanced leiturgical
5 unique
0 no data

COLUMN J: ALLOCATION ITEMS

1st digit
Produce disposition

1 all retained
2 some retained some distributed
3 all distributed
0 no data

2nd digit
Distribution item

1 produce
2 goods in kind
3 money
4 unbalanced system, no distribution
0 no data

COLUMN K: ALLOCATION CRITERIA

1st digit Gross participation	2nd digit Proprietorship	3rd digit Achievement	4th digit Office
1 produce	1 produce	1 produce	1 produce
2 goods in kind	2 goods in kind	2 goods in kind	2 goods in kind
3 money	3 money	3 money	3 money
4 none	4 none	4 none	4 none
0 no data	0 no data	0 no data	0 no data

BIBLIOGRAPHICAL REFERENCES

Bold figures are keyed to entries in the *Bibliography;* other figures are page numbers. Roman numerals, when present, are volume numbers. References are to sources of information on the particular production system in question and pertain to columns C through K. On sources for columns A and B see Murdock, *op. cit.,* or other portions of the works cited.

Summary Table

Society	A	B	C	D	E	F	G	H	I	J	K	References
ABIPON	68	131	220	00	00	21	0	935	0	00	0000	61: 110-22, 370-1
AFGHANS	31	327	110	02	22	11	1	145	3	21	4141	71: 101-2; 210: 36-8; 41: 409
			110	02	22	11	1	135	1	21	4141	71: 101-2
			110	01	21	12	1	412	1	13	4134	71: 101-2
ALEUT	51	131	221	11	11	21	2	925	1	21	4110	286: 361-3; 135: 44; 70: 248-9, 339
			321	11	11	21	2	925	1	13	4134	286: 395-6; 70: 152-3
			321	11	11	21	2	915	1	31	1114	286: 31, 385-6
			312	11	11	21	2	915	1	31	1114	286: 31, 341-4; 135: 56-7; 220: 52n2; 242: 57-8
			420	01	02	00	0	000	1	31	1144	250: 31-3
			421	11	12	21	2	915	2	14	4144	250: 31-3
			421	11	12	21	2	915	2	14	4144	250: 31-3
ANDAMANESE	38	145	221	11	11	21	2	915	1	31	1114	33: 36-7, 41-5
APALAI	64	341	110	01	22	12	1	512	1	12	2144	262: 144-5
ARANDA	44	141	221	01	10	21	2	935	0	00	0000	43: 36-9; 271: 107-8; 11: 126-7, 139, 142-4
			221	01	10	21	2	935	0	00	0000	43: 36-9; 271: 107-8; 11: 126-7, 139, 142-4
			321	11	10	21	2	915	0	00	0000	11: 127-8; 244: 231-2
			420	01	10	21	2	935	0	00	0000	11: 148-9; 43: 39-41, 119
ASHANTI	16	327	100	01	22	11	1	325	2	14	4144	187: 49; 231: 330-9; 86: 64
			100	02	22	11	1	115	1	12	2141	35: 49; 231: 114, 330-9
			200	00	02	00	1	000	1	21	4141	231: 186; 35: 49-50
ATAYAL	41	331	110	01	22	11	1	325	2	14	1144	294: 17, 34-5
			221	11	10	11	2	715	1	31	0000	294: 16, 26; 2: 3; 120: 620
			321	11	12	11	1	125	1	21	1144	294: 15-16

Summary Table (*continued*)

Society	A	B	C	D	E	F	G	H	I	J	K	References
AYMARA	66	352	110	00	22	12	1	623	1	21	1141	279: 155-7, 160-2; 155: 141ff.
			221	00	00	00	0	000	0	00	0000	280: 519-20
			321	11	12	11	1	725	1	21	1141	280: 522
			600	00	22	11	1	115	4	14	4141	155: 148-50
AZANDE	19	333	221	01	11	21	2	935	1	31	4111	157: 147-9; 31: 256; 245: 438; 73: 26, 73-4; 124: 38-9
			221	02	22	11	1	115	4	14	4141	157: 147-9; 31: 256; 124: 38-9; 39: 218-9
			321	10	22	11	1	125	1	21	4141	23: 275-6; 48: 121
BABYLONIANS	20	327	100	00	22	11	1	145	3	21	4144	56: 109-11
			100	00	11	11	1	725	1	12	4120	56: 109-11
			600	22	22	11	1	125	4	14	4141	56: 104-5
BEDOUIN	20	153	220	02	21	11	1	115	2	14	4414	230: 163-5
			520	10	10	11	2	715	0	00	0000	82: 313-4
BELU	43	324	110	01	22	12	1	522	1	21	1144	289: 31-4
BEMBA	13	337	112	21	21	12	1	522	1	12	2124	237: 145-6, 288ff.
			112	22	22	11	1	115	1	12	2140	237: 147ff., 288ff., 387-8
			220	01	11	21	1	935	1	31	0114	237: 342-50
			220	22	22	11	1	115	1	21	4141	237: 342-50
			321	10	22	11	1	125	4	14	4144	237: 329-41
BETSILEO	38	300	112	21	22	12	1	521	1	12	2144	65: 434-40
			500	01	20	12	1	521	0	00	0000	65: 469
BHOTIYAS	35	300	112	20	22	11	0	005	1	12	2142	214: 110-6
			500	01	20	12	1	521	0	00	0000	214: 51-60
BISAYAN	41	300	112	00	22	11	1	145	3	21	1144	114: 280-317, 451-4
			112	00	22	12	1	512	1	12	2144	114: 280-317, 431-5
			112	00	22	12	1	511	1	12	2144	114: 280-317, 431-5
			112	00	21	12	1	412	1	13	4134	114: 280-317, 431-5

													References
BLACKFOOT	82	151	220	01	11	21	2	935	2	1	31	4114	**114:** 505-14
			320	11	12	11	1	725	1	1	21	4141	**114:** 547-8, 586-603
			320	01	12	11	2	715	2	1	31	1144	**114:** 547-8, 586-603
			610	11	22	12	1	512	1	1	12	2142	**114:** 665-74
			610	11	21	12	1	412	1	1	13	4134	**114:** 665-74
BOLOKI	15	300	222	21	20	21	2	175	2	0	00	0000	**82:** 45-68
			222	21	20	21	2	175	2	0	00	0000	**82:** 45-68
BUKA	47	331	110	01	20	11	0	315	0	0	00	0000	**82:** 168-72
			110	11	10	21	2	935	2	0	00	0000	**82:** 168-72
			321	01	12	11	3	421	1	1	31	1144	**82:** 168-72
			612	21	22	12	1	522	3	1	13	3144	**129:** 88
			611	11	20	12	1	522	1	0	00	0000	**22:** 298-301; **130:** 356-7
													22: 327-31, 450-1
													130: 149-54
													130: 149-54
BURMESE	39	327	110	02	12	12	3	252	3	3	21	4141	**195:** 69-70; **30:** 6-8; **246:** 531-7
			110	01	22	12	1	512	4	1	14	4144	**195:** 69-70; **246:** 244-7; **30:** 7-8; **212:** 114
			310	21	11	12	2	814	1	1	13	4333	**212:** 14-18
			310	21	11	12	2	814	1	1	13	4333	**212:** 14-18
BURUSHO	35	323	110	22	22	11	3	125	3	3	31	4141	**170:** 168
			110	01	22	11	1	315	2	1	14	4144	**171:** 12; **170:** 135
			600	02	22	11	1	125	4	1	14	4141	**170:** 83-95, 168
			610	01	22	12	1	512	1	1	12	2144	**170:** 125
			720	00	12	11	1	725	1	1	12	2144	**170:** 168
CAGABA	62	351	600	01	22	12	1	502	1	1	12	2144	**235:** 1-54
			600	22	20	11	2	125	0	0	00	0000	**235:** 1-123-4
CAINGANG	60	145	221	11	22	11	2	325	2	2	14	1444	**116:** 97-105, 153-7
			621	01	22	11	1	325	1	2	14	1444	**116:** 164-6
CAMAYURA	69	341	112	21	22	12	3	421	4	1	14	4144	**207:** 17-21, 40, 45-6
			322	21	20	12	2	125	1	0	30	0000	**207:** 27-9, 40, 45-6
			600	21	20	20	3	421	0	0	00	0000	**207:** 45-6

Summary Table (*continued*)

Society	A	B	C	D	E	F	G	H	I	J	K	References
CAMBODIANS	30	327	110	02	22	11	3	155	3	21	4141	**106:** 386-7
			110	02	22	11	3	145	3	21	4141	**276:** 340
			110	01	22	12	0	511	4	14	4144	**105:** 192
			320	02	22	11	3	155	4	14	4144	**106:** 561-2
			322	11	11	11	1	725	1	13	4133	**32:** 149-50
CARIB	63	341	110	01	22	11	1	315	2	14	1144	**97:** 1-22, 133-5
			321	11	11	21	2	935	2	14	4114	**97:** 1-22, esp. 11-12
CAYAPA	66	341	110	01	22	11	1	315	2	14	4144	**203:** 281
			612	11	22	12	1	512	4	14	4144	**8:** 133-6
CHAGGA	14	334	110	02	20	11	3	145	3	00	0000	**112:** 275
			112	22	22	11	1	115	4	14	4141	**112:** 330-41
			110	01	22	11	1	125	2	14	1144	**233:** 180, 210; **112:** 383
			612	21	22	12	1	521	1	12	2142	**112:** 235-70
			610	00	11	12	1	814	2	14	4114	**112:** 235-70
			610	11	20	12	1	422	0	00	0000	**112:** 235-70
			500	11	22	12	1	521	2	14	4144	**233:** 201-3; **112:** 163
			500	00	22	11	3	155	3	21	1144	**112:** 235, 395-6
CHIGA	15	351	110	01	21	12	1	422	1	12	4124	**69:** 88-9, 99-104
			200	01	11	21	0	935	1	31	4014	**69:** 86
			620	01	22	12	1	522	1	12	2144	**69:** 85-6
			600	00	10	11	2	715	1	31	1100	**69:** 86
CHINESE	34	327	121	12	22	11	3	145	3	13	1344	**296:** 280-1; **91:** 102
			121	11	22	12	1	522	4	14	4144	**76:** 22, 36, 64-9, 144-6; **91:** 119
			121	11	20	12	1	421	1	10	0100	**76:** 144-6, 22, 36, 64-9; **91:** 119
			620	20	11	11	2	715	1	31	4111	**75:** 172-3
CHIRU	36	300	112	01	22	12	1	512	1	12	2144	**52:** 440-6
			620	00	12	11	2	715	1	31	4144	**52:** 446-9

Society												References
CHUKCHEE	33	151	510	01	20	12	1	412	1	21	0100	25: 83, 614-5
COEUR D'ALÊNE	54	141	222	21	20	21	2	175	0	00	0000	273: 101-3, 149-56
			221	11	20	11	1	125	0	00	0000	273: 101-3, 149-56
			610	00	20	11	1	125	0	00	0000	273: 60
COPPER ESKIMO	51	100	221	01	12	21	2	935	1	31	1144	133: 90, 145-52; **265:** 57-9; **132:** 86
			621	11	22	1	1	315	2	14	4144	133: 59-60
CROW	55	144	110	01	22	12	3	411	4	14	4144	177: 162
			220	01	22	21	2	175	1	31	1141	175: 357-9; **176:** 229-30
			220	01	22	21	2	175	1	31	1141	175: 357-9; **176:** 229-30
			612	21	22	12	1	512	1	12	2144	172: 88
			720	00	12	21	1	725	1	12	2144	172: 84
CUNA	61	354	110	02	20	11	1	125	0	00	0000	269: 257, 261; **188:** 90, 180-1
			110	01	22	11	1	511	4	14	4144	269: 257; **188:** 99-100, 347
			320	00	11	12	2	715	1	31	4111	59: 53-5; **269:** 21; **188:** 106-7
			612	00	12	11	2	715	1	12	2144	59: 55-6
DAHOMEANS	16	327	112	21	22	12	3	421	1	12	2142	117: 63-77
			720	01	12	11	2	715	4	14	4144	117: 101-2
DARD	35	323	221	01	10	21	2	925	0	00	0000	165: 34; **66:** 108-9
DOGON	17	341	112	21	21	12	1	422	1	13	4134	217: 131-69; **60:** 226-7
			112	21	22	12	1	623	4	14	4144	217: 131-69; **60:** 226-7; **213:** 21-3
			112	21	22	12	1	521	1	12	2144	217: 131-69; **60:** 226-7; **213:** 21-3
			320	11	10	21	0	935	0	00	0000	213: 24
			621	11	22	12	1	521	0	12	2144	**217:** 146-7
			700	01	10	11	0	715	0	00	0000	213: 25
ENGLISH	27	327	110	22	22	11	1	135	3	21	4141	20: 43-53, 92-114, 153-92
			110	22	22	11	1	115	4	14	4141	168: 32-43, 55-60
			110	22	22	11	1	145	3	12	4242	168: 32-43, 55-60
FANG	15	341	710	20	12	12	2	814	1	21	4141	44: 100, 125-6
FIJIANS	48	334	110	11	22	12	1	522	1	12	2144	226: 127-55
			610	11	22	12	4	512	4	14	4144	226: 155-64
			610	10	22	11	1	125	1	12	2144	226: 155-64

Summary Table (*continued*)

Society	A	B	C	D	E	F	G	H	I	J	K	References
FLATHEAD	54	151	220	01	22	21	2	175	1	31	1141	282: 115-21
			220	01	10	21	2	935	0	00	0000	282: 112-3, 121
			320	01	12	21	2	915	1	31	1144	282: 123-6
			610	11	22	12	1	006	1	12	2144	282: 100-1
GERMANS	27	300	110	00	20	11	1	125	0	00	0000	27: 75
GILYAK	33	145	320	01	11	21	2	925	1	31	4111	153: 1-12
			320	01	11	11	2	715	1	31	4111	152: 1-29
			320	11	22	11	1	315	2	14	4144	248: 22; **148:** 150-1
HAIDA	52	131	612	21	22	12	1	425	1	12	2142	201: 3-12; **272:** 162-70
HAITIANS	62	352	112	22	22	12	3	411	1	12	2144	118: 69-75
			112	11	22	12	1	511	4	14	4144	118: 69-75
			110	11	22	12	1	512	4	14	4144	118: 69-75
			110	11	22	12	1	512	4	14	4144	118: 69-75
HAVASUPAI	54	341	112	11	20	12	1	422	1	21	0100	260: 102-5, 211, 232
			221	11	10	21	2	935	0	00	0000	260: 110, 230
			221	00	10	21	2	905	0	00	0000	260: 110, 230
HAZARA	31	324	100	01	20	12	1	520	0	00	0000	6: 13-4, 39-40, 55
HIDATSA	55	301	110	01	22	12	3	421	1	12	2144	295: *passim.*
HOPI	58	341	112	22	22	12	3	221	1	12	2142	83: 375-6
			121	11	22	12	3	421	2	12	2142	83: 385-8; **14:** 27-31
			110	01	22	12	1	521	1	12	2144	82: 220ff.; **83:** 369, 385-8; **14:** 27-31
			421	11	22	11	2	715	1	31	1144	14: 51-5
			421	11	22	11	2	715	1	31	1444	14: 51-5
			510	01	22	12	1	511	4	14	4144	14: 49-50
			610	11	22	12	3	421	1	12	2144	14: 58-9; **197:** 100-2
HOTTENTOT	11	154	221	01	12	21	2	905	1	31	1144	243: 301-3, 316-7

Group											References
HUTSUL	28	352	221	11	20	12	1	325	0	00	0000	**243:** 293-300, 316-7
IBAN	42	341	520	11	10	11	3	715	1	10	0100	**149:** 149-55; **138:** 62-5
			610	01	22	12	1	512	1	12	2144	**149:** 187ff.; **138:** 30ff.
			112	11	22	12	1	511	4	14	4144	**104:** 46-7
			321	01	10	21	0	935	0	00	0000	**104:** 55-6
			612	21	22	11	2	715	1	31	1140	**104:** 47-9
IFALUK	46	341	100	01	22	11	1	315	2	14	4144	**34:** 37-8, 109; **51:** 27
			322	22	22	21	2	175	1	31	1141	**34:** 83L-830; **28:** 184-6
			622	11	20	12	1	411	1	12	2100	**34:** 56-63, 117-9; **151:** 92-102, 260-2, 271-2
IFUGAO	41	355	120	00	10	11	2	715	0	00	0000	**10:** 399-403; **100:** 153-79
			110	01	21	12	1	412	1	13	4134	**10:** 399-403; **100:** 153-79
			110	01	22	12	1	511	4	14	4144	**10:** 399-403; **100:** 153-79
			220	01	11	21	2	975	1	31	1114	**10:** 392-3
ILA	13	351	112	21	22	11	1	325	1	21	4144	**253:** 135-52, 386-92
			221	11	11	21	2	915	1	21	4111	**253:** 153-9, 384-6
			612	00	20	11	1	325	0	00	0000	**253:** 109-23
IRANIANS	31	327	100	22	22	11	1	135	3	21	4141	**158:** 298-302; **9:** 22; **224:** 104-5; **113:** 187-8
			100	00	11	11	2	715	1	31	4114	**158:** 367-8
			100	00	11	11	2	715	1	13	4331	**158:** 299, 367-8
			220	00	20	11	1	125	0	00	0000	**13:** 6; **93:** 36
			520	00	22	11	3	155	3	21	1144	**158:** 79-80, 350-4
			510	01	21	12	1	511	4	14	4144	**158:** 350-8
			510	01	21	12	1	412	1	12	4124	**158:** 350-8
			510	01	21	12	1	412	1	13	4134	**158:** 350-8
IROQUOIS	57	343	112	21	11	11	2	715	1	12	4221	**227:** 250-1, 257-8; **268:** 22; **178:** 15
			220	01	22	12	3	411	1	21	1141	**227:** 251-2; **99:** 371
			320	00	10	11	2	715	0	00	0000	**227:** 251
JIVARO	65	345	111	11	22	11	1	315	2	14	4144	**67:** 182; **285:** 203-4; **139:** 122-31, 183-4
			221	01	12	21	2	925	1	31	1141	**267:** 105-6; **139:** 102-7

Summary Table (*continued*)

Society	A	B	C	D	E	F	G	H	I	J	K	References
			321	01	12	21	2	915	1	31	1144	139: 179-80; 239: 603-4; 267: 104; 287: 44-5
JUKUN	18	333	112	21	21	12	1	522	1	12	4124	192: 404-14
			220	11	11	21	2	915	1	31	4111	192: 417-9
			321	11	12	21	2	915	1	31	4141	192: 421-5
			321	11	12	21	2	915	3	21	4141	192: 421
			610	11	12	21	2	915	3	31	4141	192: 425-6
KABYLES	24	343	612	21	22	12	1	522	1	12	2142	190: *passim.*
			612	21	21	12	1	422	1	13	4133	190: *passim.*
KAREN	39	351	110	01	21	12	1	412	1	13	4134	189: 75-95
			221	01	12	21	2	935	1	31	1144	189: 96
			321	11	12	21	2	935	1	31	4144	189: 106-7
KASHMIRI	36	323	100	02	22	11	1	135	3	13	4341	163: 325-31, 402, 415ff.; 198: 479
			520	00	11	11	1	725	1	12	4124	96: 169-70; 163: 361-2
			520	00	11	11	1	725	1	13	4134	96: 169-70; 163: 361-2
KAZAK	32	137	520	01	22	11	1	315	2	14	4144	82: 330-2
KIKUYU	14	311	111	11	22	12	1	511	4	14	4144	143: 55-60
			112	11	22	12	1	512	1	12	2144	143: 55-60
			612	21	22	12	1	522	1	12	2144	143: 76-84
KIPSIGIS	10	300	110	01	22	12	1	512	1	12	2144	219: 115-23
			110	00	21	12	1	412	1	13	4134	219: 115-23
KIWAI	45	341	610	21	10	21	2	935	0	00	0000	162: 11-27
KWAKIUTL	52	131	320	11	22	11	1	315	1	31	4141	101: 180-209
			610	01	22	12	1	412	1	12	2144	101: 180-209
			610	01	22	12	1	613	1	12	2144	101: 180-209
LAPPS	27	151	220	01	10	21	2	935	0	00	0000	126: 51-2, 130-1

LI	34	300	320	11	12	11	1	725	1	21	4144	**126:** **130-1**
			520	01	22	11	1	315	2	14	4144	**126:** **121-3**
			100	02	22	11	1	145	3	21	4144	209: 57-69
			111	11	21	12	1	412	1	13	4134	209: 57-69
			111	11	22	12	1	512	1	12	2144	209: 57-69
			220	01	11	21	2	935	1	31	1114	209: 56-7
			610	11	21	12	1	512	1	12	2122	209: 57
LOBI	17	341	111	11	22	12	3	411	1	12	2144	156: 130-45
			112	11	22	12	1	512	1	12	2144	156: 130-45
			222	20	22	11	1	125	1	21	1144	156: 122-4
			320	12	22	11	1	125	1	21	4141	156: 125-9
			612	21	22	12	1	522	1	12	2144	156: 152-9
			612	21	22	12	3	421	1	12	2140	156: 152-9, 264-6
MAANYAN	42	304	111	11	22	12	1	511	4	14	4144	**225**
			111	11	22	12	1	512	1	12	2144	**225**
MACASSARESE	43	323	100	00	22	11	1	125	1	12	2141	42: 103-6, 113ff.
			100	01	22	12	1	613	1	21	1144	42: 38-41
			100	22	20	12	3	202	1	13	0100	42: 110-3
			200	01	20	11	0	125	0	00	0000	42: 103-6
MALAY	30	327	322	21	12	11	1	725	1	13	4143	78
			322	21	22	11	3	155	3	13	1344	78
MALEKULANS	48	354	111	11	21	12	1	522	1	12	4124	55: 181-7
MAM	61	352	121	11	22	12	1	422	1	12	2144	290: 29, 32-44
			121	11	21	12	1	422	1	13	4134	290: 29, 32-44, 75
MANGAIANS	40	334	110	00	22	12	1	512	1	12	2144	**274:** **130-1**
			320	01	22	11	1	315	2	14	4144	**274:** **144-7**
			320	01	12	21	2	935	1	31	4141	**274:** **144-7**
			320	00	21	21	1	175	1	21	4111	**274:** **144-7**
MAORI	40	334	100	02	20	11	1	125	0	00	0000	**79**
			110	00	20	12	3	411	0	00	0000	**79**
			110	01	20	12	1	613	0	00	0000	**79**

Summary Table (*continued*)

Society	A	B	C	D	E	F	G	H	I	J	K	References
MARIA GOND	37	354	112	01	22	12	1	511	1	12	2144	109: 125-50
			222	20	02	01	1	125	3	21	4141	109: 158-60
MARICOPA	58	344	110	11	22	11	1	315	2	14	1144	261: 58-65
			221	11	10	21	2	925	0	00	0000	261: 66-7
MARSHALLESE	46	342	110	11	22	12	1	512	1	12	2144	263: 234-6
			110	22	22	11	1	135	3	21	4141	263: 78, 149, 164-9, 176
MBUNDU	12	333	111	11	22	12	1	522	1	12	2144	179: 11-2
			111	11	22	11	1	325	2	14	4144	179: 11-2
			220	10	20	11	1	125	0	00	0000	179: 13
			520	01	22	11	1	325	2	14	4144	179: 13
MEGRELIANS	29	327	110	00	22	12	1	512	1	12	2144	108: 172-3, 130-4
MENOMINI	56	246	421	11	10	21	2	715	0	00	0000	131: 1056-73
MOUNT HAGEN	45	300	110	01	22	12	1	511	1	12	2142	98: 66-7, 82-3
			620	00	20	11	0	115	4	14	4001	98: 33-5
MUONG	49	334	112	02	22	12	1	232	3	21	4141	49: 120-45, 287-94, 315-8
			220	02	21	11	1	115	1	21	4111	49: 157-9
			320	01	22	11	0	125	2	14	1044	49: 176-9
			600	22	22	12	2	125	1	31	0141	49: 115-7
			612	21	22	11	1	512	1	12	2140	49: 101-10
			612	22	22	11	1	125	1	12	2140	49: 101-10
MURNGIN	44	141	221	01	10	21	2	935	0	00	0000	292: 138-40
			321	11	10	21	2	915	0	00	0000	292: 138-9, 143
			420	01	22	12	2	616	2	14	4144	292: 138-40
MZAB	23	344	612	20	20	12	1	520	1	12	2102	193: 206-29
NAMBICUARA	69	241	112	01	20	11	0	325	0	00	0000	207: 90-2
			222	21	12	21	2	915	1	31	1144	207: 88-90

Society												References
NARON	11	141	221	10	12	21	2	935	1	31	1144	243: 76-7, 136-7, 145, 148
			420	01	12	21	2	935	1	31	1144	243: 92-3, 140-8
NAVAHO	58	341	121	11	22	12	1	512	1	12	2144	119: 28-41; 146: 5
			222	11	11	21	2	925	1	31	4111	119: 101-56
			221	11	11	21	2	925	1	31	4111	119: 101-56
			221	21	11	21	2	925	1	31	4111	119: 101-56
			222	11	22	12	1	512	4	14	4144	119: 101-56
			611									196: 489-504
NUER	10	346	110	01	22	12	1	512	1	12	2144	72: 84, 91, 180
NUPE	18	323	110	02	20	11	1	115	0	00	0000	204: 241-50, 59
			110	02	22	12	1	412	1	13	3144	204: 241-56
			110	21	22	12	1	512	4	14	4144	204: 241-56
			110	01	20	11	1	325	1	21	0000	204: 241-56
			700	11	12	11	2	715	1	12	2144	204: 256-7, 277-8, 289-92
			700	10	11	11	2	715	1	13	4134	204: 256-7, 277-8, 289-92
NYORO	15	327	700	00	11	11	1	725	1	13	4134	44: 117-8
			700	00	12	11	1	725	1	12	2144	44: 117-8
OJIBWA	56	141	220	01	22	11	1	315	2	14	4144	134: 4-6; 7: 16; 256: 12-13
			421	11	22	21	2	175	1	31	1144	57: 128; 159: 93-6
			420	01	22	11	1	315	2	14	4144	159: 126
ONA	67	141	221	00	10	21	2	935	1	31	1000	111: I: 271-2
			621	11	22	11	1	315	2	14	1144	111: I: 194-5
OSSET	29	336	110	02	22	11	1	135	3	21	4141	150: 143-5
			110	02	22	11	1	145	3	21	4141	150: 143-5
			500	02	11	11	3	715	1	13	4134	150: 146-9
OTORO	19	311	112	21	22	12	1	522	1	12	2144	205: 40-57
			221	21	12	21	2	915	1	21	1041	205: 58-9
			522	21	22	11	3	715	1	31	4144	205: 59-65
PAIUTE	54	141	221	11	11	21	2	925	2	31	4111	174: 197
			221	11	11	21	2	925	1	31	4111	141: 83

Summary Table (*continued*)

Society	A	B	C	D	E	F	G	H	I	J	K	References
PAPAGO	59	341	221	11	11	21	2	925	1	31	4111	141: 81-2
			222	21	11	21	2	925	1	31	4111	141: 88; 174: 284
			420	01	12	21	2	935	2	14	4144	141: 100; 174: 201-3
PATWIN	53	101	112	20	22	12	1	520	1	21	1144	40: 125-80; 283: 104ff.
			621	20	20	11	2	125	1	31	0000	40: 159-60
PENOBSCOT	57	344	221	11	20	11	1	325	1	31	1404	181: 243-5; 259: 34-48, 203ff
			200	00	10	11	2	715	0	00	0000	181: 243-5; 259: 34-48, 246-8
			321	00	20	21	2	175	1	31	1100	259: 90, 203ff.
POPOLUCANS	50	302	110	11	22	12	1	512	4	14	4144	89: 21, 35
PUKAPUKANS	49	341	110	12	22	11	1	125	1	21	4141	15: 36-50
			110	11	22	11	1	325	2	14	4144	15: 36-50
			110	11	22	11	0	105	3	21	1141	15: 58-9, 66-7, 281-2
			322	22	22	12	1	522	1	12	2144	15: 76-7
			610	11	22	12	3	421	1	12	2142	15: 77-9
			610	11	22	12	3	421	1	12	2142	
RIFFIANS	24	354	110	11	22	12	1	006	1	12	2144	47: 54-5
ROMANS	25	327	120	22	21	12	1	232	3	21	4111	278: 277-82; 37: 259-60, 451-2, 561-2; 115
			120	22	21	12	1	232	3	13	4333	278: 277-82; 37: 259-60, 451-2, 561-2; 115
			120	22	22	12	3	242	1	13	3143	278: 277-82; 37: 259-60, 451-2, 561-2; 115
			120	22	22	12	3	242	1	21	4141	278: 277-82; 37: 259-60, 451-2, 561-2; 115
SAMOANS	49	334	110	11	10	11	2	715	0	00	0000	191: 287-8
			610	20	22	12	3	411	0	12	2144	191: 287-9
			600	20	20	12	0	225	0	00	0000	191: 289-91
SAMOYED	33	151	510	01	22	12	1	511	1	21	4141	127: 150-1, 163, 197
SANPOIL	54	101	222	21	11	21	2	925	1	31	4114	234: 77-92

SAXONS	27	327	320	11	12	11	2	715	1	31	1141	234: 69-71
			421	11	10	21	2	915		00	0000	234: 98
			111	01	22	12	1	511	4	14	4144	247: 117-25
			110	02	02	01	1	135	3	21	4141	247: 117-25, 235
SEMANG	30	145	420	01	12	21	2	935	2	14	4144	82: 11-23
SINKAIETK	54	151	221	11	10	21	2	915	0	00	0000	223: 19-20
			622	21	12	21	2	915	2	14	1144	223: 12-3
SIRIONO	65	341	100	01	22	11	1	315	2	14	4144	122: 29
			221	11	12	21	2	935	1	31	1144	122: 25-7, 33
SOMALI	21	353	112	22	20	11	1	115	0	00	0000	166: 72-3, 76-7
			112	21	20	12	3	411	1	12	0100	166: 72-3, 76-7
			200	21	10	11	2	715	0	00	0000	166: 75-6
SONGHAI	22	323	110	01	22	12	1	511	1	12	2144	241: 19-20
SOTHO	12	337	221	22	22	11	1	115	3	21	4141	38: 179-83
TAHITIANS	40	334	110	20	20	11	3	135	3	20	0000	82: 211-2
			610	01	22	12	1	421	1	12	2142	82: 215
TALLENSI	17	341	112	20	22	12	1	623	1	12	2144	87: 237-61
			112	20	21	12	1	422	1	12	4121	87: 237-61
TAOS	58	341	110	01	22	12	1	613	1	12	2144	216: 18
			220	01	20	11	0	115	0	00	0000	216: 19; 194: 37
			520	12	22	11	2	115	2	14	4144	216: 72; 194: 33
TARAHUMARA	59	351	112	21	22	12	1	412	1	13	3144	21: 26-30
			112	11	22	12	1	512	1	12	2144	21: 26-30
			500	11	20	11	1	315	1	31	0000	21: 10-3
			621	11	22	12	1	512	1	12	2144	21: 50-5
TARASCO	50	337	112	22	22	11	1	155	3	21	4144	17: 20-5, 47, 63-5; 88
			112	22	22	11	1	145	3	21	4144	17: 20-5, 47, 63-5; 88
			112	20	21	12	3	412	1	13	4134	17: 20-5, 47, 63-5; 88
			520	01	21	11	1	315	1	33	4134	17: 30-1; 88
			720	01	11	11	1	725	1	13	4134	17: 33-47; 88

Summary Table (*continued*)

Society	A	B	C	D	E	F	G	H	I	J	K	References
TELUGU	37	322	110	01	22	12	1	412	1	21	1144	64: 78-9, 85-6
			110	01	21	12	1	412	1	12	4124	64: 78-9, 85-6
TENETEHARA	60	341	111	11	22	12	1	613	1	13	4143	291: 31-50
			220	01	10	21	2	915	0	00	0000	291: 57
TERENA	68	331	111	11	22	11	1	315	2	11	4144	208: 10-11
			221	00	11	21	2	905	1	31	1114	208: 10, 13
THAI	30	327	112	01	21	12	1	412	1	13	4134	107: II: 9-14; **299:** 199-208
			112	01	22	12	1	511	1	12	2144	19: 19-20; **107:** II: 9-14; **299:** 198-205
			110	02	22	12	1	232	3	21	4141	284; 11; **277:** 676-7; **19:** 5
			112	02	22	12	3	252	3	13	1343	299: 199-205; **107:** II: 9-14; **284:** 11; 277: 676-7; **19:** 5
			110	02	20	11	1	125	0	00	0000	299: 126; 19: 24; **277:** 600
			222	21	10	11	2	715	1	21	0101	264; **161:** 243-4
			321	01	21	12	1	412	1	13	4134	107: II: 40-4; **277:** 477-8, 604; **299:** 183
THONGA	12	303	110	01	22	12	1	522	1	12	2144	137: II: 20-31
			110	02	22	11	1	115	1	12	2144	137: I: 331, 405-7, II: 20-31
TIBETANS	35	327	112	22	22	11	1	135	3	21	4141	46: 123-4; **18:** 302-3
			112	22	22	11	1	135	3	13	1343	46: 123-4; **18:** 302-3; **180:** 123; **53:** 190; 95: 121-34
			112	01	22	12	1	512	4	14	4144	3: 74, 76-7
			112	01	21	12	1	412	1	13	4134	3: 74; **50:** 221
			110	00	22	11	1	125	4	14	4144	229: 24; **95:** 121-34
TIGRE	21	233	100	22	20	11	1	115	0	00	0000	215: II: 191
TIKOPIA	49	331	111	11	22	12	1	613	2	14	1144	80: 66-8, 134
			421	11	20	12	2	613	0	00	0000	81: 92-4
			610	11	20	12	1	512	1	12	0100	80: 134
			612	21	21	12	1	006	1	12	2122	80: 117-33

TIMBIRA	60	215	112	20	22	12	1	421	1	12	2140	**206:** 57-64, 94ff.
			600	01	22	12	1	421	1	12	2140	**206:** 40, 94ff.
TIV	18	344	112	01	22	12	3	421	4	14	4144	**68:** 83-4; **1:** 212
			110	01	20	12	1	421	1	12	2144	**26:** 46-9, 50-1; **63:** 25
			110	01	20	12	1	623	1	12	2100	**26:** 46-9, 50-1
			110	01	11	11	1	165	0	00	0000	**26:** 45-6, 50-1
			221	11	11	21	0	915	1	31	1010	**1:** 224-5
TROBRIANDERS	47	334	110	02	22	11	1	115	1	12	2144	**184:** 156-63; **185:** 87-93, 157-8
			112	01	22	12	3	411	1	12	2144	**184:** 156-63; **185:** 87-93, 157-8
			112	01	22	12	1	512	1	12	2144	**184:** 156-63; **185:** 87-93, 157-8
			112	01	22	12	1	512	1	12	2144	**184:** 156-63; **185:** 87-93, 157-8
			112	01	22	12	1	512	1	12	2144	**184:** 156-63; **185:** 87-93, 157-8
			612	22	22	11	1	125	1	12	2142	**184:** 124-56, 415-6
TRUMAI	69	341	321	11	10	21	1	915	1	21	0000	**202:** 25-7
TUAREG	23	324	500	02	22	11	1	165	3	21	4144	**167:** 164-79, 254-60
TUBATULABAL	53	141	221	11	12	21	2	905	2	14	4141	**288:** 12-3, 50-1
TUPINAMBA	60	351	110	01	22	12	1	512	1	12	2144	**254:** 319; **275:** 211; **36:** 426
TURKANA	10	315	522	21	22	12	2	425	1	31	4141	**110:** 44-8, 124-32
			522	21	22	11	2	715	2	14	4141	**110:** 44-8, 124-32
WAPISHANA	63	341	221	11	20	11	0	125	0	00	0000	**74:** 51-2, 87
			321	11	22	11	0	125	2	14	1040	**74:** 59-61, 87
WINNEBAGO	56	344	222	21	22	21	2	175	1	31	4041	**228:** 111-4
WINTUN	53	151	221	21	21	21	2	175	1	31	4110	**103:** 401-6
			421	12	12	21	2	935	2	14	1144	**103:** 408-9
			621	01	12	21	2	915	1	12	2141	**103:** 422-3
WOGEO	45	345	110	02	22	11	1	115	4	14	4144	**121:** 299-300
			110	01	20	12	1	613	0	00	0000	**121:** 286-97
			421	11	20	12	1	510	0	00	0000	**121:** 309-11
WOLOF	22	327	112	00	22	12	1	412	1	12	2144	**92:** 29-35
			100	02	20	11	1	105	0	00	0000	**92:** 29-35, 55-7

Summary Table (*continued*)

Society	A	B	C	D	E	F	G	H	I	J	K	References
YAGUA	65	341	221	11	22	11	2	325	1	31	1144	77: 40-2
			621	10	22	11	2	325	2	14	4144	77: 30-2
YAMI	41	341	320	00	12	11	2	715	1	31	4141	2: 3
YAQUI	59	341	200	01	12	21	2	905	1	31	1440	16: 14
YOKUTS	53	151	220	02	22	11	1	115	4	14	4144	94: 163
			401	11	20	11	2	325	2	14	4144	94: 178
			600	11	22	11	1	325	2	14	4144	94: 161
ZULU	12	327	222	00	21	11	2	115	1	31	4110	144: 315-20; **145**: 15-6
ZUNI	58	341	110	11	21	12	3	421	1	12	4122	102: 314-7; **266**: 350
			422	21	20	11	2	715	0	00	0000	**266**: 354-61

BIBLIOGRAPHY

Sources of Empirical Data

Numbers are keyed to the Summary Table in the Appendix

1. Abraham, Roy Clive. *The Tiv People.* Lagos: The Government Printer, 1933.
2. Asai, Erin. "Social Structure of the Tribes in Formosa." Unpublished lecture given at Yale University, 1950.
3. Asboe, Walter. "Agricultural Methods in Lahoul, Western Tibet," *Man* (London), XXXVII (1937), 74-77.
4. ————. "Farmers and Farming in Ladakh (Tibetan Kashmir)," *Journal of the Royal Central Asian Society,* XXXIV (1947), 186-192.
5. Auscher, E. S. *A History and Description of French Porcelain.* London: Cassell, 1905.
6. Bacon, Elizabeth Emaline. "The Hazara Mongols: A Study in Social Organization." Dissertation submitted in partial satisfaction of the degree of Ph.D. in Anthropology in the Graduate Division. University of California, August 9, 1951.
7. Barnouw, Victor. *Acculturation and Personality among the Wisconsin Chippewa.* (Memoir 72, American Anthropological Association.) Menasha, Wis., 1950.
8. Barrett, S. A. *The Cayapa Indians of Ecuador.* (Indian Notes and Monographs, No. 40.) New York: Heye Foundation, 1925.
9. Barth, Fredrick. *Principles of Social Organization in Southern Kurdistan.* (Universitets Etnografiske Museum Bulletin, No. 7.) Oslo: Brodrene Jorgensen, 1953.
10. Barton, R. F. Pages 385-446, plates 38-45, in *Ifugao Economics.* (University of California Publications in American Archaeology and Ethnology, XV, No. 5.) Berkeley: University of California Press, 1922.
11. Basedow, Herbert. *The Australian Aboriginal.* Adelaide: F. W. Preece and Sons, 1925.
12. Baumann, Hermann. "The Division of Work According to Sex in African Hoe Culture," *Africa,* I (1928), 289-319.
13. Bawer, Mahmud. *The Kuhgalu of Iran.* Unpublished manuscript received by Human Relations Area Files from Henry Field, 1954.

14. Beaglehole, Ernest. *Notes on Hopi Economic Life*. (Yale University Publications in Anthropology, No. 15.) New Haven, 1937.

15. Beaglehole, Ernest, and Pearl Beaglehole. *Ethnology of Pukapuka*. (Bernice P. Bishop Museum Bulletin 150.) Honolulu, 1938.

16. Beals, Ralph L. *The Aboriginal Culture of the Cahita Indians*. (Ibero-Americana, No. 19.) Berkeley: University of California Press, 1943.

17. ————. *Cheran: A Sierra Tarascan Village*. (Smithsonian Institution, Institute of Social Anthropology, Publication No. 2.) Washington: U. S. Government Printing Office, 1946.

18. Bell, Sir Charles. *The People of Tibet*. Oxford: Clarendon Press, 1928.

19. Benedict, Ruth. "Thai Culture and Behavior." (Data Paper No. 4, Southeast Asia Program, Department of Far Eastern Studies, Cornell University.) Unpublished study, September 1943.

20. Bennett, H. S. *Life on the English Manor: A Study of Peasant Conditions, 1150-1400*. New York: Macmillan, 1938.

21. Bennett, Wendell C., and Robert M. Zingg. *The Tarahumara*. Chicago: University of Chicago Press, 1935.

22. Blackwood, Beatrice. *Both Sides of Buka Passage*. Oxford: Clarendon Press, 1935.

23. Bloss, J. F. E. "The Sudanese Angler," *Sudan Notes and Records*, XXVI, 257-281. Khartoum: McCorquodale, 1945.

24. Blunt, E. A. H. *The Caste System of Northern India*. London: Oxford University Press, 1931.

25. Bogoras, Waldemar. *The Chukchee*. In three parts. (Memoirs of the American Museum of Natural History, XI.) Leiden: E. J. Brill; and New York: G. E. Stechert, 1904, 1907, 1909.

26. Bohannan, Laura, and Paul Bohannan. *The Tiv of Central Nigeria*. London: International African Institute, 1953.

27. Boissonade, P. *Life and Work in Medieval Europe*. (Trans., Eileen Power.) New York: Alfred A. Knopf, 1927.

28. Born. [sic] "Einige Beobachtungen ethnographischer Natur über die Oleai-Inseln," *Mitteilungen aus den Deutschen Schutzgebeiten* (Berlin), XVII (1904), 175-191.

29. Bowen, Richard LeBaron, Jr. "The Dhow Sailor," *The American Neptune* (Salem, Mass.), IX (1951), 161-202.

30. Brant, Charles. "Tadagale: A Burmese Village in 1950." (Data Paper No. 13, Southeast Asia Program, Department of Far Eastern Studies, Cornell University.) Ithaca, 1954.

31. Brock, R. G. C. "Some Notes on the Zande Tribe as Found in the

Meridi District (Bahr El Ghazal Province)," *Sudan Notes and Records*, I, 249-262. Cairo: The French Institute of Oriental Archaeology, 1918.

32. Brodrick, Alan Houghton. *Little Vehicle: Cambodia and Laos.* London: Hutchinson, [1948].

33. Brown, A. R. *The Andaman Islanders.* Cambridge: University Press, 1922.

34. Burrows, Edwin Grant. "The People of Ifaluk: A Little-Disturbed Atoll Culture." Unpublished manuscript submitted as a final report, Coordinated Investigation of Micronesian Anthropology, Pacific Science Board, National Research Council. Washington, [1949].

35. Busia, K. A. *The Position of the Chief in the Modern Political System of Ashanti: A Study of the Influence of Contemporary Social Changes on Ashanti Political Institutions.* London: Oxford University Press for the International African Institute, 1951.

36. Cardim, Fernão. *A Treatise of Brasil and Articles touching the dutie of the Kings Majestie our Lord, and to the common good of all the estate of Brasil.* Hakluytus Posthumus or Purchas His Pilgrimes, XVI, 417-517. Glasgow: James MacLehose and Sons, 1906. (Data from 1583-1625.)

37. Cary, Max. *A History of Rome.* London: Macmillan, 1935.

38. Casalis, E. *Les Bassoutos.* Paris: Librairie de Ch. Meyrueis, 1859.

39. Casati, Gaetano. *Ten Years in Equatoria and the Return with Emin Pasha*, I. London and New York: Frederick Warne, 1891.

40. Castetter, Edward F., and Willis H. Bell. *Pima and Papago Indian Agriculture.* Albuquerque: University of New Mexico Press, 1942.

41. Cervin, Vladimir. "Problems in the Integration of the Afghan Nation," *Middle East Journal*, VI (1952), 400-416.

42. Chabot, H. Th. *Verwantschap, Stand en Sexe in Zuid-Celebes.* Groningen: J. B. Wolters' Uitgeversmaatschappij, 1950.

43. Chewings, Charles. *Back in the Stone Age: The Natives of Central Australia.* Sydney: Angus and Robertson, 1936.

44. Cline, Walter. *Mining and Metallurgy in Negro Africa.* (General Series in Anthropology, No. 5.) Menasha, Wis.: George Banta, 1937.

45. Collins, Henry Bascom. "The Islands and Their People." Pages 1-30 in *The Aleutian Islands: Their People and Natural History.* (Smithsonian Institution War Background Studies, No. 21.) Washington, 1945.

46. Combe, G. A. (ed.). *A Tibetan on Tibet.* [A report of the travels and observations of one Paul Sherap.] London: T. Fisher Unwin, 1926.

47. Coon, Carleton S. *Tribes of the Rif.* (Harvard African Studies, IX.) Cambridge: Peabody Museum, 1931.

48. Costermans, Basiel. "Abstract 391: Yitri: La pêche au poison chez les peuplades de l'Uele, *Kongo-Overzee*, 15, 3/4, 129-54, 1949," *African Abstracts*, I, 121. London: International African Institute, 1950.

49. Cuisinier, Jeanne. *Les Mu'ò'ng.* (Travaux et Mémoires de l'Institut d'Ethnologie, No. 45.) Paris: Institut d'Ethnologie, 1948.

50. Cunningham, Alexander. *Ladak, Physical, Statistical and Historical, with Notices of the Surrounding Countries.* London: Wm. H. Allen, 1854.

51. Damm, Hans, *et al. Zentralkarolinen, Part II: Ifaluk, Aurepik, Faraulip, Sorol, Mogemog.* (Ergebnisse der Südsee-Expedition 1908-1910, Section B, Vol. X, Part 2.) Hamburg: Friederichsen, De Gruyter, 1938.

52. Das, Jarak Chandra. "Some Notes on the Economic and Agricultural Life of a Little Known Tribe on the Eastern Frontier of India," *Anthropos*, XXXII (1937), 440-449. (Deals with the Chiru.)

53. Das, Sarat Chandra. *Journey to Lhasa and Central Tibet.* (Ed., W. W. Rockhill.) London: John Murray, 1902.

54. Davidson, D. S. "The Family Hunting Territory in Australia," *American Anthropologist*, XXX (1928), 614-631.

55. Deacon, A. Bernard. *Malekula: A Vanishing People in the New Hebrides.* London: George Routledge and Sons, 1934.

56. Delaporte, L. *Mesopotamia.* New York: Knopf, 1925.

57. Densmore, Frances. *Chippewa Customs.* (Bureau of American Ethnology, Bulletin No. 86.) Washington: Government Printing Office, 1929.

58. ————. *Music of the Tule Indians of Panama.* (Smithsonian Miscellaneous Collections, LXXVII, No. 11.) Washington, 1926.

59. DeSmidt, Leon S. *Among the San Blas Indians of Panama.* Troy, 1948.

60. Desplagnes, Lt. Louis. *Le Plateau Central Nigérien.* Paris: Emile Larose, 1907.

61. Dobrizhoffer, Martin. *An Account of the Abipones.* 3 vols. London: John Murray, 1822.

62. Dollard, John. *Caste and Class in a Southern Town.* (3rd ed.) New York: Doubleday, 1957.

63. Downes, R. M. *The Tiv Tribe.* Kaduna: The Government Printer, 1933.

64. Dube, S. C. *Indian Village.* Ithaca: Cornell University Press, 1955.

65. DuBois, H. M., S. J. *Monographie des Betsileo.* (Travaux et Mémoires de l'Institut d'Ethnologie, No. 34.) Paris: Institut d'Ethnologie, 1938.

66. Durand, Algernon. *The Making of a Frontier.* London: John Murray, 1900.

67. Dyott, George Miller. *On the Trail of the Unknown in the Wilds of Ecuador and the Amazon.* London: Thornton Butterworth, 1926.

68. East, Rupert (ed.) *Akiga's Story: The Tiv Tribe as Seen by One of Its Members.* London: The International Institute of African Languages and Cultures, Oxford University Press, 1939.

69. Edel, May Mandelbaum. *The Chiga of Western Uganda.* New York: Oxford University Press, 1957.

70. Elliott, Henry Wood. *Our Arctic Province.* New York: Charles Scribner's Sons, 1886.

71. Engert, Cornelius van H. *A Report on Afghanistan.* (Department of State, Division of Publications, Series C, No. 53.) Washington, 1924.

72. Evans-Pritchard, E. E. *The Nuer.* Oxford: Clarendon Press, 1940.

73. ————. *Witchcraft, Oracles, and Magic among the Azande.* Oxford: Clarendon Press, 1937.

74. Farabee, William Curtis. *The Central Arawaks.* (University of Pennsylvania, The University Museum, Anthropological Publications, IX.) Philadelphia: The University Museum, 1918.

75. Fei, Hsiao-Tung. *Peasant Life in China.* New York: Oxford University Press, 1946.

76. Fei, Hsiao-Tung, and Chang, Chih-i *Earthbound China: A Study of Rural Economy in Yunnan.* Chicago: University of Chicago Press, 1945.

77. Fejos, Paul. *Ethnography of the Yagua.* New York: The Viking Fund, 1943.

78. Firth, Raymond. *Malay Fishermen: Their Peasant Economy.* London: Kegan Paul, Trench, Trubner, 1946.

79. ————. *Primitive Economics of the New Zealand Maori.* New York: Dutton, 1929.

80. ————. *Primitive Polynesian Economy.* London: George Routledge and Sons, 1939.

81. ————. *We, the Tikopia.* London: George Allen and Unwin, 1936.

82. Forde, C. Daryll. *Habitat, Economy, and Society.* New York: E. P. Dutton, 1934.

83. ————. "Hopi Agriculture and Land Ownership," *Journal of the Royal Anthropological Institute,* XLI (1931), 357-405.

84. ————. "Land and Labour in a Cross River Village, Southern Nigeria," *Geographical Journal,* XC (1937), 24-51.

85. Fortes, Meyer. "Communal Fishing and Fishing Magic in the Northern Territories of the Gold Coast," *Journal of the Royal Anthropological Institute of Great Britain and Ireland,* LXVII (1937), 131-142.

86. ————. "Time and Social Structure: An Ashanti Case Study." Pages 54-84 in Meyer Fortes (ed.), *Social Structure: Studies Presented to A. R. Radcliffe-Brown.* London: Oxford University Press, 1949.

87. Fortes, M., and S. L. Fortes. "Food in the Domestic Economy of the Tallensi," *Africa,* IX (1936), 237-276.

88. Foster, George M. *Empire's Children.* (Smithsonian Institution, Institute of Social Anthropology, Publication No. 6.) Mexico: Imprenta Nuevo Mundo, 1948.

89. ————. *A Primitive Mexican Economy.* (Monographs of the American Ethnological Society, No. 5.) New York: J. J. Augustin, 1942.

90. Francotte, Henri. *L'Industrie dans la Gréce ancienne.* 2 vols. Liège: Imprimerie H. Vaillant-Carmanne, 1900-1901.

91. Fried, Morton H. *Fabric of Chinese Society.* New York: Prager, 1953.

92. Gamble, David P. *The Wolof of Senegambia.* London: International African Institute, 1957.

93. Garrod, Oliver. "The Nomadic Tribes of Persia To-day," *Journal of the Royal Central Asian Society* (London), XXX (1946), Part I, 32-46.

94. Gayton, A. H. *Yokuts and Western Mono Ethnography.* (Anthropological Records, X, No. 2.) Berkeley: University of California Press, 1948.

95. *Gazetteer of the Kangra District.* Vol. II: "Kulu, Lahaul and Spiti." Calcutta: Punjab Government, 1883-1884.

96. Gervis, Pearce. *This Is Kashmir.* London: Cassell, 1954.

97. Gillin, John. *The Barama River Caribs of British Guiana.* (Papers of the Peabody Museum of American Archaeology and Ethnology, XIV, No. 2.) Cambridge, 1936.

98. Gitlow, Abraham L. *Economics of the Mount Hagen Tribes, New Guinea.* (Monographs of the American Ethnological Society, No. 12.) New York: J. J. Augustin, 1947.

99. Goldenweiser, A. A. "On Iroquois Work." Pages 365-372 in *Summary Report of the Geological Survey of Canada*. Ottawa Department of Mines, 1913.

100. Goldman, Irving. "The Ifugao of the Philippine Islands." Pages 153-179 in Mead, *Cooperation and Competition among Primitive Peoples*, q. v.

101. ————. "The Kwakiutl of Vancouver Island." Pages 180-209 in Mead, *Cooperation and Competition among Primitive Peoples*, q. v.

102. ————. "The Zuni Indians of New Mexico." Pages 313-353 in Mead, *Cooperation and Competition among Primitive Peoples*. q. v.

103. Goldschmidt, Walter. Pages 303-443 in *Nomlaki Ethnography*. (University of California Publications in American Archaeology and Ethnology, XLII, No. 4.) Berkeley: University of California Press, 1951.

104. Gomes, Edwin H. *Seventeen Years among the Sea Dyaks of Borneo*. London: Seeley, 1911.

105. Goudal, Jean. *Labour Conditions in Indo-China*. (International Labour Office, Studies and Reports, Series B, No. 26.) Geneva, 1938.

106. Gourou, Pierre. *Land Utilization in French Indochina*. (Trans., Guest, Clark, and Pelzer.) Washington: Institute of Pacific Relations, 1945.

107. Graham, W. A. *Siam*. 2 vols. London: Alexander Moring, The De La More Press, 1924.

108. Grigolia, Alexander. *Custom and Justice in the Caucasus*. Philadelphia: University of Pennsylvania, 1939.

109. Grigson, W. V. *The Maria Gonds of Bastar*. London: Oxford University Press, 1938.

110. Gulliver, P. H. *The Family Herds*. London: Routledge and Kegan Paul, 1955.

111. Gusinde, Martin, S. V. D. *Die Feuerland-Indianer*. 1. Band: "Die Selk'nam." Wien: Verlag der Internationalen Zeitschrift "Anthropos," 1931.

112. Gutmann, Bruno. Pages 1-733 in *Das Recht der Dschagga*. (Arbeiten zur Entwicklungpsychologie, No. 7.) Muenchen: C. H. Beck, 1926. (Translated as "Chagga Law" by A. M. Nagler for HRAF. Page citations are to the translation.)

113. Hadary, Gideon. "The Agrarian Problem in Iran," *Middle East Journal*, V (1951), 181-196.

114. Hart, Donn V. "Barrio Caticugan: A Visayan Filipino Community." Unpublished dissertation submitted in partial ful-

166

fillment of the requirements for the degree of Doctor of Social Science in the Graduate School. Syracuse University, May 1954.

115. Heitland, William E. *Agricola.* Cambridge: University Press, 1921.

116. Henry, Jules. *Jungle People.* New York: J. J. Augustin, 1941.

117. Herskovits, Melville J. *Dahomey: An Ancient West African Kingdom.* 2 vols. New York: J. J. Augustin, 1938.

118. ————. *Life in a Haitian Valley.* New York: Alfred A. Knopf, 1937.

119. Hill, W. W. Pages 1-101 in *The Agricultural and Hunting Methods of the Navaho Indians.* (Yale University Publications in Anthropology, No. 18.) New Haven: Yale University Press, 1938.

120. Hofmann, Amerigo. "Aus Formosa," *Geographischen Gesellschaft in Wien,* LV, 600-638. Wien: R. Lechner, 1912.

121. Hogbin, H. Ian. "Tillage and Collection in a New Guinea Economy," *Oceania,* IX (1938-1939), 127-151, 286-325.

122. Holmberg, Allan R. *Nomads of the Long Bow: The Siriono of Eastern Bolivia.* (Smithsonian Institution, Institute of Social Anthropology Publication No. 10.) Washington: U. S. Government Printing Office, 1950.

123. Honda, Seirkou. "Eine Besteigung des Mount Morrison auf der Insel Formosa," *Mitteilungen der Deutschen Gesellschaft für Natur- und Völkerkunde Ostasiens,* VI, 469-473. Berlin: Asher, 1897.

124. Hutereau, Armand. *Notes sur la vie familiale et juridique de quelques populations du Congo Bèlge.* (Annales du Musée du Congo Bèlge, Ethnographie et Anthropologie, Serie 3: Documents Ethnographiques concernant les Populations du Congo Bèlge, Vol. I, Pt. 1.) Bruxelles: Ministre des Colonies, 1909.

125. Hutton, J. H. *Caste in India: Its Nature, Function, and Origins.* (2d ed.) Bombay: Oxford University Press, 1951.

126. Indiana University. *The Lapps.* Subcontractor's Monograph, HRAF-3, Indiana-6, prepared for the Human Relations Area Files in 1955. In typescript.

127. ————. *The Samoyed.* Subcontractor's Monograph, HRAF-13, Indiana-49, prepared for HRAF in 1955. In typescript.

128. Ivanov, S. V. "Aleut Hunting Headgear and its Ornamentation," *Proceedings of the Twenty-third International Congress of Americanists,* pp. 477-504. New York, 1930.

129. Ivens, Walter G. *The Island Builders of the Pacific.* London: Seeley, Service, 1930.

130. ————. *Melanesians of the South-east Solomon Islands.* London: Kegan Paul, Trench, Trubner, 1927.

131. Jenks, Albert Ernest. *The Wild Rice Gatherers of the Upper Lakes: A Study in American Primitive Economics.* (Bureau of American Ethnology, 19th Annual Report, 1897-1898, pp. 1013-1137.) Washington: Government Printing Office, 1900.

132. Jenness, Diamond. "The Copper Eskimos," *Geographical Review,* IV (1917), 81-91.

133. ————.*The Life of the Copper Eskimos.* (Report of the Canadian Arctic Expedition, 1913-18, Vol. XII, Pt. a.) Ottawa: F. A. Acland, 1922.

134. ————. *The Ojibwa Indians of Parry Island, Their Social and Religious Life.* (Bulletin of the Canada Department of Mines, No. 78.) Ottawa National Museum of Canada, 1935.

135. Jochelson, Waldemar. *History, Ethnology and Anthropology of the Aleut.* Washington: Carnegie Institute of Washington, 1933.

136. ————. *The Yakut.* (Anthropological Papers of the American Museum of Natural History, XXXIII, Part II, 33-225.) New York, 1933.

137. Junod, Henri A. *The Life of a South African Tribe.* 2 vols. London: Macmillan, 1927.

138. Kaindl, R. F. *Die Huzulen.* Wien, 1894.

139. Karsten, Rafael. *The Head-Hunters of Western Amazonas: The Life and Culture of the Jibaro Indians of Eastern Ecuador and Peru.* (Societas Scientiarum Fennica: Commentationes Humanarum Litterarum, VII, No. 1.) Helsingfors: Centraltryckeriet, 1935.

140. Kawaguchi, Ekai. *Three Years in Tibet.* Adyar, Madras: The Theosophist Office, 1909.

141. Kelly, Isabel T. Pages 67-210, plates 17-22 in *Ethnography of the Surprise Valley Paiute.* (University of California Publications in American Archaeology and Ethnology, XXXI, No. 3.) Berkeley, 1934.

142. Kennan, George. *Tent Life in Siberia, and Adventures among the Koraks and Other Tribes in Kamtchatka and Northern Asia.* New York: G. P. Putnam and Sons, 1870.

143. Kenyatta, Jomo. *Facing Mount Kenya: The Tribal Life of the Gikuyu.* London: Secker and Warburg, 1937.

144. Kidd, Dudley. *The Essential Kafir.* London: Adam and Charles Black, 1904.

145. ————. *Kafir Socialism.* London: Adam and Charles Black, 1908.

146. Kimball, Solon T., and John A. Provinse. *Navaho Social Organization in Land Use Planning.* Manuscript taken from *Applied Anthropology,* I (July-September 1942), No. 4.

147. Kluckhohn, Clyde, and Dorothea Leighton. *The Navaho.* Cambridge: Harvard University Press, 1946.

148. Knox, Thomas W. *Overland through Asia.* Hartford: American Publishing Company, 1870.

149. Koenig, Samuel. "The Ukrainians of Eastern Galicia." Unpublished Ph.D. dissertation. Yale University, 1935.

150. Kovalevskii, Maksim M. *Coutume contemporaine et Loi ancienne.* Paris: Librairie du Recueil General des Lois et des Arrets, 1893.

151. Krämer, Augustin Friedrich. *Zentralkarolinen, Part I: Lamotrek Gruppe, Oleai, Feis.* (Ergebnisse der Südsee-Expedition 1908-1910, Vol. X, Pt. 1.) Hamburg: Friederichsen, De Gruyter, 1937.

152. Kreinovich, E. A. "Morskoi promysel giliakov derevni Kul'" ("The Fishing Industry of the Gilyaks in the Village Kul'"), *Sovetskaia Etnografiia,* 1934, No. 5, 78-96. Leningrad: Akademia Nauk SSSR, 1934.

153. ————. "Okhota na belukhu u giliakov derevni Puir" ("Hunting of the Beluga by the Gilyaks of the Village Puir") *Sovetskaia Etnografiia,* 1935, No. 2, 108-115. Moskva: Akademia Nauk SSSR, 1935.

154. Kroeber, A. L. *Handbook of the Indians of California.* (Bureau of American Ethnology, Bulletin 78.) Washington: Government Printing Office, 1925.

155. LaBarre, Weston. *The Aymara Indians of the Lake Titicaca Plateau, Bolivia.* (American Anthropological Association, Memoir No. 68.) 1948.

156. Labouret, Henri. *Les Tribus du Rameau Lobi.* (Travaux et Mémoires de l'Institut d'Ethnologie, No. 15) Paris: Institut d'Ethnologie, 1931.

157. Lagae, C. R. *Les Azande ou Niam-Niam: L'organisation Zande, croyances religieuses et magiques, coutumes familiales.* (Bibliotheque-Congo, XVIII.) Bruxelles: Vromant, 1926.

158. Lambton, Ann K. S. *Landlord and Peasant in Persia.* London: Oxford University Press, 1953.

159. Landes, Ruth. "The Ojibwa of Canada." Pages 87-126 in Margaret Mead (ed.), *Cooperation and Competition among Primitive Peoples.* New York and London: McGraw-Hill, 1937.

160. ————. *Ojibwa Sociology.* (Columbia University Contributions

to Anthropology, XXIX.) New York: Columbia University Press, 1937.

161. Landon, Kenneth P. *Thailand in Transition: A Brief Survey of Cultural Trends in the Five Years since the Revolution of 1932.* Distributed in the U. S. by the University of Chicago Press, Chicago. [1939].

162. Landtman, Gunnar. *Papuan Magic in the Building of Houses.* (Acta Academiae Aboensis Humaniora, I, No. 5.) Abo: Abo Akademi, 1920.

163. Lawrence, Walter R. *The Valley of Kashmir.* London: Henry Frowde, Oxford University Press Warehouse, 1895.

164. Leighton, Alexander H., and Dorothea C. Leighton. *The Navaho Door: An Introduction to Navaho Life.* Cambridge: Harvard University Press, 1944.

165. Leitner, G. W. *Dardistan in* 1866, 1886, and 1893. England: Oriental University Institute. Woking, [1893?].

166. Lewis, I. M. *Peoples of the Horn of Africa.* London: International African Institute, 1955.

167. Lhote, Henri. *Les Touaregs du Hoggar.* Paris: Payot, 1944.

168. Lipson, E. *The Economic History of England.* Vol. I. London: Adam and Charles Black, 1945.

169. ————. *The History of the Woolen and Worsted Industries.* London: Adam and Charles Black, 1921.

170. Lorimer, David L. "The Supernatural in the Popular Belief of the Gilgit Religion," *Journal of the Royal Asiatic Society of Great Britain and Ireland,* 1929, 507-536.

171. Lorimer, Emily Overend. "The Burusho of Hunza," *Antiquity,* XII, 5-15. Gloucester: John Bellows, 1938.

172. Lowie, Robert H. *The Crow Indians.* New York: Farrar and Rhinehart, 1935.

173. ————. *Military Societies of the Crow Indians.* (Anthropological Papers of the American Museum of Natural History, XI, Part III, 143-217.) New York, 1913.

174. ————. *Notes on Shoshonean Ethnography.* (Anthropological Papers of the American Museum of Natural History, XX, Pt. III, 185-314.) New York, 1924.

175. ————. *The Religion of the Crow Indians.* (Anthropological Papers of the American Museum of Natural History, XXV, 309-444.) New York, 1922.

176. ————. *Social Life of the Crow Indians.* (Anthropological Papers of the American Museum of Natural History, IX, Part II, 179-248.) New York, 1912.

177. ————. *The Tobacco Society of the Crow Indians*. (Anthropological Papers of the American Museum of Natural History, XXI, Part II, 101-200.) New York, 1919.

178. Lyford, Carrie A. *Iroquois Crafts*. (Publications of the United States Indian Service, Indian Handicraft Pamphlets, No. 6.) Lawrence, Kansas: Haskell Institute, 1945.

179. McCulloch, Merran. *The Ovimbundu of Angola*. London: International African Institute, 1952.

180. MacDonald, David. *The Land of the Lama*. London: Seeley, Service, 1929.

181. McKern, W. C. *Functional Families of the Patwin*. (University of California Publications in American Archaeology and Ethnology, XIII, No. 7, 235-258.) Berkeley: University of California Press, 1922.

182. McKim, Fred. *San Blas: An Account of the Cuna Indians of Panama*. (Etnologiska Studier, XV.) Göteborg, 1947.

183. MacLeod, William Christie. "The Family Hunting Territory and Lenape Political Organization," *American Anthropologist*, XXIV (1922), 448-463.

184. Malinowski, Bronislaw. *Argonauts of the Western Pacific*. London: George Routledge and Sons, 1922.

185. ————. *Coral Gardens and Their Magic*. 2 vols. London: George Allen and Unwin, 1935.

186. ————. *The Family among the Australian Aborigines*. London: University of London Press, 1913.

187. Manoukian, Madeline. *Akan and Ga-Adangme Peoples of the Gold Coast*. (Ethnographic Survey of Africa, Part I: Western Africa.) London: Oxford University Press for the International African Institute, 1950.

188. Marshall, Donald Stanley. "Cuna Folk: A Conceptual Scheme involving the Dynamic Factors of Culture, as applied to the Cuna Indians of Darien." Unpublished manuscript presented to the Department of Anthropology in partial fulfillment of the requirements for the A.B. degree with Honors. Harvard University, [1950].

189. Marshall, H. I. *The Karen People of Burma: A Study in Anthropology and Ethnology*. (The Ohio State University Bulletin, XXVI, No. 13.) Columbus: The University of Ohio Press, 1922.

190. Maunier, René. *La Construction collective de la Maison en Kabylie*. (Travaux et Mémoires de l'Institut d'Ethnologie, No. 3.) Paris: Institut d'Ethnologie, 1926.

191. Mead, Margaret. "The Samoans." Pages 282-312 in Mead, *Co-operation and Competition among Primitive Peoples*, q. v.

192. Meek, C. K. *A Sudanese Kingdom.* London: Kegan Paul, Trench, Trubner, 1931.

193. Mercier, Marcel. *La Civilisation urbaine au Mzab.* Alger: Imprimerie Administrative et Commerciale Emile Pfister, 1922.

194. Miller, Merton L. *A Preliminary Study of the Pueblo of Taos New Mexico.* Chicago: University of Chicago Press, 1898.

195. Mi Mi Khiang. *Burmese Family.* Calcutta: Longmans Green, 1946.

196. Mindeleff, Cosmos. *Navaho Houses.* (Bureau of American Ethnology, 17th Annual Report, Part 2, 1895-1896, 470-517.) Washington: Government Printing Office, 1898.

197. Mindeleff, Victor. *A Study of Pueblo Architecture: Tusayan and Cibola.* (8th Annual Report, Bureau of Ethnology.) Washington: Government Printing Office, 1891.

198. Modi, Jivanji Jamshedji. "The Pundits of Kashmir," *Journal of the Anthropological Society of Bombay*, X (1913, 1914, 1915, and 1916), 461-485. Bombay, 1917.

199. Moninger, M. M. "The Hainanese Miao," *Journal of the North China Branch of the Royal Asiatic Society*, LII, 40-50. Shanghai, 1921.

200. Morgan, Lewis H. *League of the Ho-De-No-Sau-Nee or Iroquois.* 2 vols. New Haven: Human Relations Area Files, 1954.

201. Murdock, George Peter. *Rank and Potlatch among the Haida.* (Yale University Publications in Anthropology, No. 13.) New Haven, 1936.

202. Murphy, Robert F. and Buell Quain. *The Trumai Indians of Central Brazil.* (American Ethnological Society, Bulletin 24.) Locust Valley, N. Y.: J. J. Augustin, 1955.

203. Murra, John. "The Cayapa and Colorado." Pages 277-284 in Julian H. Steward (ed.), *Handbook of South American Indians.* (Smithsonian Institution, Bureau of American Ethnology, Bulletin 143.) Washington: Government Printing Office, 1948.

204. Nadel, S. F. *A Black Byzantium: The Kingdom of Nupe in Nigeria.* London: Oxford University Press, 1942.

205. ————. *The Nuba.* London: Oxford University Press, 1947.

206. Nimuendaju, Curt. *The Eastern Timbira.* Berkeley: University of California Press, 1946.

207. Oberg, Kalervo. *Indian Tribes of Northern Mato Grosso, Brazil.* (Smithsonian Institution, Institute of Social Anthropology, Publication No. 15.) Washington: Government Printing Office, 1953.

208. ————. *The Terena and the Cuduveo of Southern Mato Grosso, Brazil.* (Smithsonian Institution. Institute of Social Anthropology, Publication No. 9.) Washington: Government Printing Office, 1949.

209. Odaka, Kunio. *Economic Organization of the Li Tribes of Hainan Island.* (Trans., Mikiso Hane.) (Yale Southeast Asia Studies, Translation Series.) New Haven, 1950.

210. Office Suisse Commerciale. Cervinka, M. Vladimir. *Afghanistan.* (Office Suisse D'Expansion Commerciale, Rapport special No. 58, Série A.) Lausanne, 1950.

211. Orleans, Prince Henri d'. *Around Tonkin and Siam.* London: Chapman and Hall, 1894.

212. Orr, Kenneth G. *Field Notes on the Burmese Standard of Living as Seen in the Case of a Fisherman-Refugee Family.* (Notes of the Burma Community Research Project, Department of Anthropology, University of Rangoon.) Rangoon, 1951. Mimeographed.

213. Palau Marti, Montserrat. *Les Dogon.* Paris: Presses Universitaires de France, 1957.

214. Pant, S. D. *The Social Economy of the Himalayans.* London: George Allen and Unwin, 1935.

215. Parkyns, Mansfield. *Life in Abyssinia.* Vol. II. New York: D. Appleton, 1854.

216. Parsons, Elsie Clews. *Taos Pueblo.* (General Series in Anthropology, No. 2.) Menasha, Wis.: George Banta, 1936.

217. Paulme, Denise. *Organisation sociale des Dogon.* Paris: Editions Domat-Montchrestien, 1940.

218. Pelham, H. F. *Essays on Roman History.* Oxford: Clarendon Press, 1911.

219. Peristianis, Jean-G. *La Vie et le Droit coutoumier des Kipsigis du Kenya.* Paris: Les Editions Domat-Montchrestien, 1938.

220. Petroff, Ivan. *Report of the Population, Industries, and Resources of Alaska.* (Census Office, Tenth Census of the Uinted States, 1880, Special Reports.) Washington: Department of Interior, 1884.

221. Popov, A. A. "Olenvodstvo u dolgan" ("Reindeer Breeding among the Dolgan"), *Sovetskaia Etnografiia,* 1935, Pt. 4-5, 184-205. Moskva and Leningrad: Akademia Nauk SSSR, 1935.

222. Porée, Guy, and Eveline Maspero. *Moeurs et Coutumes des Kmèrs.* Paris: Payot, 1938.

223. Post, Richard H. "The Subsistence Quest." In W. Cline *et al., The Sinkaietk or Southern Okanagon of Washington.* (Gen-

eral Series in Anthropology, No. 6.) Menasha, Wis.: George Banta, 1938.

224. Price, M. Phillips. "The Present Situation in Persia," *Journal of the Royal Central Asian Society,* XXXVIII (1951), 102-111.

225. Provinse, John H. "Cooperative Ricefield Cultivation among the Siang Dyaks of Central Borneo," *American Anthropologist,* XXXIX (1937), 77-102.

226. Quain, Buell. *Fijian Village.* Chicago: University of Chicago Press, 1948.

227. Quain, B. H. "The Iroquois." Pages 240-281 in Margaret Mead (ed.), *Cooperation and Competition among Primitive Peoples.* New York: McGraw-Hill, 1937.

228. Radin, Paul. *The Winnebago Tribe.* (37th Annual Report of the Bureau of American Ethnology, 1915-1916.) Washington: Government Printing Office, 1923.

229. Ramsay, H. *Western Tibet: A Practical Dictionary of the Language and Customs of the Districts Included in the Ladak Wazarat.* Lahore: W. Ball, 1890.

230. Raswan, Carl R. *Black Tents of Arabia.* New York: Creative Age Press, 1947.

231. Rattray, R. S. *Ashanti Law and Constitution.* Oxford: Clarendon Press, 1929.

232. ————. *Religion and Art in Ashanti.* Oxford: Clarendon Press, 1927.

233. Raum, O. F. *Chaga Childhood: A Description of Indigenous Education in an East African Tribe.* London: Oxford University Press for the International Institute of African Languages and Cultures, 1940.

234. Ray, Verne F. *The Sanpoil and Nespelem: Salishan Peoples of Northeastern Washington.* (University of Washington Publications in Anthropology, V, December 1932.) Seattle: University of Washington Press, 1933.

235. Reichel-Dolmatoff, Gerardo. *Los Kogi.* 2 vols. (Revista del Instituto Etnologico Nacional, IV.) Bogota, Colombia: Editorial Iqueima, 1949-50.

236. Richards, Audrey I. *Hunger and Work in a Savage Tribe.* London: George Routledge and Sons, 1932.

237. ————. *Land, Labour and Diet in Northern Rhodesia: An Economic Study of the Bemba Tribe.* New York: Oxford University Press, 1939.

238. Rivers, W. H. R. *The Todas.* London and New York: Macmillan, 1906.

239. Rivet, Paul. "Les Indiens Jibaros: Etude géographique, historique et ethnographique," *L'Anthropologie*, XVIII (1907), 333-369, 583-618.

240. Rockhill, William Woodville. "Notes on the Ethnology of Tibet." Pages 665-747, 52 plates, in *Report of the U. S. National Museum for 1893*. Washington: Smithsonian Institution, 1895.

241. Rouch, Jean. *Les Songhay*. Paris: Presses Universitaires de France, 1954.

242. Sarytschew, Gawrila. *Account of a Voyage of Discovery to the Northeast of Siberia, the Frozen Ocean, and the North-east Sea*. Vol. II. London: Richard Phillips, 1806.

243. Schapera, I. *The Khoisan Peoples of South Africa*. London: George Routledge and Sons, 1930.

244. Schulze, Louis. "The Aborigines of the Upper and Middle Finke River: Their Habits and Customs, with Introductory Notes on the Physical and Natural-History Features of the Country," *Transactions and Proceedings and Report of the Royal Society of South Australia*, XIV, 210-246. Adelaide: W. C. Rigby, 1891.

245. Schweinfurth, Georg. *The Heart of Africa: Three Years' Travels and Adventures in the Unexplored Region of Central Africa from 1868 to 1871*. Vol. I, 434-559; Vol. II, 3-35. New York: Harper and Brothers, 1874.

246. Scott, Sir James George. *The Burman: His Life and Notions*. London: Macmillan, 1910.

247. Seebohm, Frederic. *The English Village Community*. (4th ed.) London: Longmans, Green, 1905.

248. Seeland, Nicolas. "Die Ghiliaken: Eine ethnographische Skizze," *Russische Revue*, XXI, 97-130, 222-254. St Petersburg: Carl Röttger, 1882.

249. Seligman, Charles Gabriel, and Brenda Z. Seligman. *The Veddas*. Cambridge: University Press, 1911.

250. Shade, Charles I. "Ethnological Notes on the Aleuts." Unpublished manuscript submitted in accordance with requirements for the degree of A.B. with distinction. Harvard University, Department of Anthropology, [1949].

251. Shen, T. H. *Agricultural Resources of China*. Ithaca: Cornell University Press, 1951.

252. Shen, Tsung-lien, and Shen-chi Liu. *Tibet and the Tibetans*. Stanford, Cal.: Stanford University Press, 1953.

253. Smith, Edwin W., and Andrew M. Dale. *The Ila-speaking Peoples of Northern Rhodesia*. Vol. I. London: Macmillan, 1920.

254. Soares de Souza, Gabriel. *Tratado descriptivo do Brasil em 1587.*

175

(Revista do Instituto Historico e Geographico do Brazil, XIV, 1-423.) Rio de Janeiro, 1851.

255. Speck, Frank G. "The Family Hunting Band as the Basis of Algonkian Social Organization," *American Anthropologist*, V (1915), 289-305.

256. ————. *Family Hunting Territories and Social Life of Various Algonkian Bands of the Ottawa Valley.* (Canada, Department of Mines, Geological Survey, Memoir 70, No. 8, Anthropological Series.) Ottawa: Government Printing Bureau, 1915.

257. ————. "Family Hunting Territories of the Lake St. John Montagnais and Neighboring Bands," *Anthropos*, XXII (1927), 387-403.

258. ————. "Mistassini Hunting Territories in the Labrador Peninsula," *American Anthropologist*, XXV (1923), 452-471.

259. ————. *Penobscot Man.* Philadelphia: University of Pennsylvania Press, 1940.

260. Speir, Leslie. *Havasupai Ethnography.* (Anthropological Papers, XXIX, Part 3.) New York: American Museum of Natural History, 1928.

261. ————. *Yuman Tribes of the Gila River.* Chicago: University of Chicago Press, 1933.

262. Speiser, Felix. *Im Düster des Brasilianischen Urwalds.* Stuttgart: Strecker und Schröder, 1925.

263. Spoehr, Alexander. *Majuro: A Village in the Marshall Islands.* (Fieldiana: Anthropology, XXXIX.) Chicago: Natural History Museum, 1949.

264. Srichandrakumara, Phya Indra Montri. "Adversaria of Elephant Hunting (together with an account of all the rites, observances and acts of worship to be performed in connection therewith, as well as notes on vocabularies of spirit language, fake or taboo language and elephant command words)," *Journal of the Siam Society*, XXIII, 61-96. Bangkok: Bangkok Times Press, 1929.

265. Stefánsson, Viljálmur. *The Stefánsson-Anderson Arctic Expedition of the American Museum: Preliminary Ethnological Report.* (Anthropological Papers of the American Museum of Natural History, XIV, Pt. 1.) New York, 1914.

266. Stevenson, Matilda Coxe. *The Zuni Indians.* (23rd Annual Report, Bureau of American Ethnology.) Washington: Government Printing Office, 1904.

267. Stirling, Matthew Williams. *History and Ethnographical Material on the Jivaro Indians.* (Bureau of American Ethnology, Bulletin 117.) Washington: Smithsonian Institution, 1938.

176

268. Stites, Sara Henry. *Economics of the Iroquois.* Ph.D. dissertation, Bryn Mawr College. Lancaster, Pa.: The New Era Printing Company, 1905.

269. Stout, David B. "The Cuna." Pages 257-268 in *Handbook of South American Indians,* IV. (Smithsonian Institution, Bureau of American Ethnology, Bulletin 143.) Washington: U. S. Government Printing Office, 1948.

270. ————. *San Blas Cuna Acculturation: An Introduction.* (Viking Fund Publications in Anthropology, No. IX.) New York, 1947.

271. Strehlow, Theodor Georg Heinrich. *Aranda Traditions.* Carlton: Melbourne University Press, 1947.

272. Swanton, J. R. *Contributions to the Ethnology of the Haida.* (Memoirs of the American Museum of Natural History, VIII, Part 1.) New York: G. E. Stechert, 1905.

273. Teit, James A. "The Salishan Tribes of the Western Plateau." Pages 23-294 in *Forty-fifth Annual Report of the Bureau of American Ethnology to the Secretary of the Smithsonian Institution, 1927-1928.* Washington: Government Printing Office, 1930.

274. Te Rangi Hiroa. (P. H. Buck). *Mangaian Society.* (Bernice P. Bishop Museum, Bulletin 122.) Honolulu, 1934.

275. Thevet, André. *Les singularitez de la France antarctique, autrement nommé Amerique: et isles decouvertes de nostre temps.* (Nouvelle édition, ed., Paul Gaffarel.) Paris: Maisonneuve, 1878. (Data from 1555.)

276. Thompson, Virginia. *French Indo-China.* New York: Macmillan, 1937.

277. ————. *Thailand: The New Siam.* New York: Macmillan, 1941.

278. Toutain, Jules. *The Economic Life of the Ancient World.* New York: Alfred A. Knopf, 1930.

279. Tschopik, H., Jr. *The Aymara.* (Anthropological Papers, No. 44.) New York: American Museum of Natural History, 1951.

280. ————. "The Aymara." Pages 501-573 in Julian H. Steward (ed.), *Handbook of South American Indians,* II. (Smithsonian Institution, Bureau of American Ethnology, Bulletin 143.) Washington: Government Printing Office, 1946.

281. Tumin, Melvin M. *Caste in a Peasant Society.* Princeton: Princeton University Press, 1952.

282. Turney-High, Harry Holbert. *The Flathead Indians of Montana.* (Memoirs of the American Anthropological Association No. 46.) Menasha, Wis., 1936.

283. Underhill, Ruth. *Social Organization of the Papago Indians.* New York: Columbia University Press, 1939.

284. United Nations. *Draft Report on Cooperatives in Thailand.* Prepared in Rural Welfare Division, Food and Agriculture Organization, July, 1949.

285. Up de Graff, Fritz W. *Head Hunters of the Amazon: Seven Years of Exploration and Adventure.* New York: Duffield, 1923.

286. Veniaminov, Ivan Evsieevich Popov. *Zapiski ob ostrovakh Unalishkinskago otdela.* St. Petersburg: Russian-American Company, 1840. (Trans. for HRAF by B. Keen.)

287. Vigna, Juan. "Bosquejo Sobre los Indios Shuaras o Jibaros," *America Indigena,* V (1945), 35-49.

288. Voegelin, Erminie W. *Tubatulabal Ethnography.* (Anthropological Records, II, No. 1.) Berkeley: University of California Press, 1938.

289. Vroklage, B. A. G., S. V. D. *Ethnographie der Belu in Zentral-Timor.* Erster teil. Leiden: E. J. Brill, 1953.

290. Wagley, Charles. *Economics of a Guatemalan Village.* (Memoirs of the American Anthropological Association, No. 58.) Menasha, Wis., 1941. (On Santiago Chimaltenango Village.)

291. Wagley, Charles, and Eduardo Galvao. *The Tenetehara Indians of Brazil.* New York: Columbia University Press, 1949.

292. Warner, W. Lloyd. *A Black Civilization.* New York: Harper and Bros., 1937.

293. Waterfield, O. "Tiv Fishing Party," *Nigeria,* No. 26, 408-411. Lagos, 1947.

294. Wiedfeldt, O. "Wirtschaftliche, rechtliche und soziale Grundtatsachen und Grundformen der Atayalen auf Formosa," *Mitteilungen der Deutschen Gesellschaft für Natur- und Völkerkunde Ostasiens,* 15 Pt., C: 7-55. Tokyo, 1914.

295. Wilson, Gilbert Livingstone. *Agriculture of the Hidatsa Indians.* University of Minnesota, November 1917.

296. Winfield, Gerald F. *China: The Land and the People.* New York: William Sloane Associates, 1948.

297. Wissler, Clark. *Material Culture of the Blackfoot Indians.* (Anthropological Papers, American Museum of Natural History, V, Part 1, 1910.)

298. Wyckaert, R. P., P. B. "Forgerons païens et Forgerons chrétiens au Tanganika," *Anthropos,* IX (1914), 371-380.

299. Young, Ernest. *The Kingdom of the Yellow Robe.* Westminster: Archibald Constable, 1898.

178

General Works

Anderson, E. H., and G. T. Schwenning. *The Science of Production Organization.* New York: John Wiley and Sons, 1938.

Apple, Dorrian. "The Social Structure of Grandparenthood," *American Anthropologist,* LVIII (1956), 656-663.

Blau, Peter M. *Bureaucracy in Modern Society.* New York: Random House, 1956.

Bücher, Carl. *Arbeit und Rhythmus.* Leipzig: Bei Hirzel, 1896.

—————. *Industrial Evolution.* (Trans., from the 3rd German ed., S. M. Wickett.) New York: Henry Holt, 1912.

Buxton, L. H. Dudley. *Primitive Labour.* London: Methuen, 1924.

Cottrell, Fred. *Energy and Society.* New York: McGraw-Hill, 1955.

Curwen, E. Cecil, and Gudmund Hatt. *Plough and Pasture: The Early History of Farming.* New York: Henry Schuman, 1953.

Dale, Ernest. *Planning and Developing the Company Organization Structure.* (American Management Association, Research Report No. 20.) New York, 1952.

Davie, Maurice R. *The Evolution of War.* New Haven: Yale University Press, 1929.

Davis, Kingsley. *Human Society.* New York: Macmillan, 1949.

Davis, Ralph Currier. *The Influence of the Unit of Supervision and the Span of Executive Control on the Economy of Line Organization Structure.* (Bureau of Research, Monograph No. 26.) Columbus: Ohio State University Press, 1941.

DeJong, Albert. *Die Menselijke Factor in de Bedrijfshuishouding en de Bedrijfseconomische Problematiek.* Leiden: H. E. Stenfert Kroese, 1954.

Descamps, Paul. "L'Atelier chez les Sauvages," Instituts Solvay, *Revue de l'Institut de Sociologie,* I (1923-1924), 351-378.

—————. *Etat social des Peuples sauvages: Chasseurs—Pêcheurs—Cueilleurs.* Paris: Payot, 1930.

—————. "Le Role social de la Cueillette," Instituts Solvay, *Revue de l'Institut de Sociologie,* I (1925-1926), Nos. 2-3, 241-264.

Driver, Harold E. *An Integration of Functional, Evolutionary, and Historical Theory by Means of Correlations.* (Indiana University Publications in Anthropology and Linguistics, XXII, No. 1, Memoir 12.) Indiana University, 1956.

Einzig, Paul. *Primitive Money.* London: Eyre and Spottiswoode, 1949.

179

Firth, Raymond. *Elements of Social Organization.* London: Watts, 1951.

————. "Some Features of Primitive Industry," *Economic Journal, Economic History Series,* No. 1 (1926), 13-22.

Forde, C. Daryll. *Habitat, Economy, and Society.* New York: E. P. Dutton, 1934.

Frazer, Sir James George. *The Golden Bough.* (Abridged ed.) New York: Macmillan, 1931.

Freeman, Linton C., and Robert F. Winch. "Societal Complexity: An Empirical Test of a Typology of Societies," *American Journal of Sociology,* LXII (1957), 461-466.

Friedmann, Georges. *Industrial Society.* (Trans., Spaulding and Sheppard.) Glencoe: Free Press, 1955.

Goldhamer, Herbert, and E. A. Shils. "Types of Power and Status," *American Journal of Sociology,* XLV (1939), 171-178.

Goode, William J. *Religion among the Primitives: The Web of Religion and Sex, Economics, Politics.* Glencoe: Free Press, 1951.

Goodfellow, D. M. *Principles of Economic Sociology.* London: George Routledge and Sons, 1939.

Graicunas, V. A. "Relationship in Organization." Pages 183-187 in Gulick and Urwick, *op. cit. infra.*

Gras, N. S. B. *Industrial Evolution.* Cambridge: Harvard, 1930.

Greaves, I. C. *Modern Production among Backward Peoples.* London: George Allen and Unwin, 1935.

Grosse, Ernst. *Die Formen der Familie und die Formen der Wirtschaft.* Leipzig: J. C. B. Mohr, 1896.

Gulick, Luther, and L. Urwick (eds.). *Papers on the Science of Administration.* New York: Institute of Public Administration, 1937.

Hahn, Eduard. *Die Entstehung der Pflugkultur.* Heidelberg: C. Winter, 1909.

Hamilton, Sir Ian. *The Soul and Body of an Army.* London: Arnold, 1921.

Herskovits, Melville J. *Economic Anthropology.* New York: Alfred A. Knopf, 1952.

————. *The Economic Life of Primitive Peoples.* New York: Knopf, 1940.

Hobhouse, L. T.; G. C. Wheeler; and M. Ginsberg. *The Material Culture and Social Institutions of the Simpler Peoples.* London: Chapman and Hall, 1930.

Hobson, John A. *Work and Wealth: A Human Valuation.* New York: Macmillan, 1914.

Homans, George C. *The Human Group.* New York: Harcourt Brace, 1950.

180

Ireson, William G., and Eugene L. Grant (eds.). *Handbook of Industrial Engineering and Management*. Englewood Cliffs: Prentice-Hall, 1955.

Kendall, M. P. "The Problem of the Chief Executive," *Bulletin of the Taylor Society*, VII, No. 2.

Kochen, Manfred, and Marion J. Levy. "The Logical Nature of an Action Scheme," *Behavioral Science*, I (1956), 265-289.

Kover, Arthur J. "Some Factors Affecting the Span of Control in Bureaucratic Organizations." Unpublished paper, Yale University, 1957.

Kropotkin, Petr. *Mutual Aid*. Boston: Extending Horizons Books, 1955.

Levy, Marion J., Jr. *The Structure of Society*. Princeton: Princeton University Press, 1952.

Lewis, Oscar. "Comparisons in Cultural Anthropology." Pages 259-292 in *Yearbook of Anthropology*. New York: Wenner-Gren Foundation, 1955.

Linton, Ralph. *The Study of Man*. New York: Appleton-Century, 1936.

Lippert, Julius. *Kulturgeschichte der Menschheit*. Stuttgart: F. Enke, 1886-1887.

Lowie, Robert H. "The Buffalo Drive and an Old-World Hunting Practice," *Natural History*, XXIII (1923), 280-282.

—————. *Primitive Society*. New York: Boni and Liveright, 1925.

Maine, Sir Henry Sumner. *Lectures on the Early History of Institutions*. New York: Henry Holt, 1888.

—————. *Village-Communities in the East and West*. New York: Henry Holt, 1889.

Malinowski, Bronislaw. *Magic, Science, and Religion*. Garden City: Doubleday, 1954.

Maunier, René. *Introduction à la Sociologie*. Paris: Alcan, 1929.

Mead, Margaret (ed.). *Cooperation and Competition among Primitive Peoples*. New York and London: McGraw-Hill, 1937.

Miller, Delbert C., and William H. Form. *Industrial Sociology*. New York: Harper and Bros., 1951.

Moore, Omar K. "Divination—A New Perspective," *American Anthropologist*, LIX (1957), 69-74.

Moore, Wilbert E. *Economy and Society*. Garden City: Doubleday, 1955.

—————. *Industrialization and Labor*. Ithaca: Cornell University Press, 1951.

—————. *Industrial Relations and the Social Order*. (Revised ed.) New York: Macmillan, 1951.

————. Unpublished syllabus of lectures in Industrial Sociology. Princeton University, 1954.

Murdock, George Peter. *Outline of World Cultures.* New Haven: Human Relations Area Files, 1954.

————. *Social Structure.* New York: Macmillan, 1949.

————. "World Ethnographic Sample," *American Anthropologist,* LIX (1957), 664-687.

Murdock, George P.; Clellan S. Ford; et al. *Outline of Cultural Materials.* New Haven: Human Relations Area Files, 1950.

Nieboer, H. J. *Slavery as an Industrial System.* The Hague: Martinus Nijhoff, 1900.

Parsons, Talcott, and E. A. Shils. *Toward a General Theory of Action.* Cambridge: Harvard, 1951.

Parsons, Talcott, and Neil J. Smelser. *Economy and Society.* Glencoe: Free Press, 1956.

Quiggin, A. Hingston. *A Survey of Primitive Money.* London: Methuen, 1949.

Salisbury, Richard F. "Asymmetrical Marriage Systems," *American Anthropologist,* LVIII (1956), 687-715.

Sayce, R. U. *Primitive Arts and Crafts.* Cambridge: University Press, 1933.

Schmidt, Max. *Grundriss der ethnologischen Volkswirtschaftslehre.* 2 vols. Stuttgart: Ferdinand Enke, 1920-1921.

Schuessler, Karl F., and Harold E. Driver. "A Factor Analysis of Sixteen Primitive Societies," *American Sociological Review,* XXI (1956), 493-499.

Simmel, Georg. *Conflict* and *The Web of Group Affiliations.* (Trans., Wolff and Bendix.) Glencoe: Free Press, 1955.

Simmons, Leo. *The Role of the Aged in Primitive Societies.* New Haven: Yale University Press, 1945.

Sumner, William Graham, and Albert Galloway Keller. *The Science of Society.* 4 vols. New Haven: Yale University Press, 1927.

Taylor, Frederick Winslow. *Shop Management.* New York: Harper and Bros., 1911.

Thurnwald, Richard. *Economics in Primitive Communities.* Oxford: Oxford University Press, 1932.

Tilgher, Adriano. *Work: What It Has Meant to Men through the Ages.* (Trans., Fisher.) London: George G. Harrap, 1931.

Udy, Stanley H., Jr. " 'Bureaucratic' Elements in Organizations: Some Research Findings," *American Sociological Review,* XXIII (1958), 415-420.

182

————. "The Organization of Production in Nonindustrial Culture." Unpublished doctoral dissertation. Princeton University, Department of Economics and Sociology, 1958.

————. "The Structure of Authority in Nonindustrial Production Organization," *American Journal of Sociology,* forthcoming.

Urwick, L. "Organization as a Technical Problem." Pages 49-88 in Gulick and Urwick, *op. cit. supra.*

Viljoen, Stephan. *The Economics of Primitive Peoples.* London: Staples Press, 1936.

Weber, Max. *From Max Weber: Essays in Sociology.* (Trans. and ed., Gerth and Mills.) New York: Oxford University Press, 1946.

————. *General Economic History.* (Trans., Frank H. Knight.) Glencoe: Free Press, 1950.

————. *The Theory of Social and Economic Organization.* (Trans., A. M. Henderson and Talcott Parsons.) New York: Oxford University Press, 1947.

Whiting, John. "The Cross Cultural Method." Pages 523-531 in G. Lindzey (ed.), *Handbook of Social Psychology.* Cambridge: Addison-Wesley, 1954.

Whiting, John, and Irving Child. *Child Training and Personality: A Cross-cultural Study.* New Haven: Yale University Press, 1953.

Wittfogel, Karl A. *Oriental Despotism: A Comparative Study of Total Power.* New Haven: Yale University Press, 1957.